The Dreamer's Guide to
Living in France

JOHN HODGKINSON

The Dreams, The Realities

Dreamer's Guides^{TM}
Breese Books, London

Published in 1995 by Dreamer's Guides™
Breese Books Limited
164 Kensington Park Road
London W11 2ER

© John Hodgkinson, 1995

ISBN: 0 947533 66 4

This book is dedicated to the people of Parcé sur Sarthe
who have proved, during the floods of 1995, to be
true neighbours.

Typeset in 10 / 12pt Palatino and Ottawa by
Ann Buchan (Typesetters) Middlesex
Printed in Great Britain by
Itchen Printers Limited, Southampton

CONTENTS

CHAPTER ONE

THE DREAM

A brilliant flash of electric blue streaked across the river. It was closely followed by another and they both turned to orange as a pair of kingfishers swooped up to favourite perches overlooking the water. A family of ducks paddled quietly under the overhanging branches along the river-bank while overhead a group of swallows and martins were giving a breathtaking display as they wrought havoc among the midges and mosquitoes. We had left the roar of the weir behind us and were steaming gently upstream, afloat for the first time on our river. There wasn't another boat in sight and dragonflies flitted across the surface in tandem as they ensured the survival of their species. The scenery was gorgeous, the sun was shining, use of the river was free and at the end of the trip we would be moored up outside our own house. The forthcoming evening would be spent dining superbly to the strains of Bach or Vivaldi under the shade of an old acacia tree at a favourite restaurant not three miles away.

This was our dream coming true; a house with a mooring for our boat at a price we could afford without a loan from the IMF. But it was in France. The dream had matured over several years — starting to germinate during a holiday in 1981 when, without any prior thought or planning, we had crossed the channel (and experienced at first hand the dubious pleasure of being surrounded by seasick passengers on a cross-Channel ferry) to take a holiday in Normandy. We had enjoyed delicious meals of seafood, near empty roads, even emptier rivers and all the sights, sounds, tastes and smells of France. Now it had come true and we were the proud owners of our very own little bit of France and able to enjoy to the full the delights of life over the water. Breakfast had been hot *croissants* straight from the village *boulangerie*, a *baguette* of delicious French bread just out of the oven with farm-fresh butter. We had been woken by the clock tower bells ringing the Angelus at eight o'clock, to throw open the shutters and look out across the river and the weir from which was rising a light veil of condensation rapidly evaporating as it met the warmth of the rising sun. The poplars which lined the opposite bank, and were reflected in the mirror of the still water, had been planted some 15 years or so ago to mark the birth of a daughter to the owner of the riverside meadow, and in another five years might be felled to pay for her wedding.

Our dream had been for a holiday home — a modest little house which we could lock up and leave and which would be a base for our steamboating and some gastronomy and general relaxation; yours may be similar or maybe you have it in mind to make the break and become a permanent French resident after, or even before, retirement. Perhaps you hope to make a little money by letting your French house to holidaymakers. Whatever the reasons behind your dream you will be attracted by *La Vie Française* — the space, the weather, the wine, the food and, above all, the ambience and the people will appeal to you. You will probably speak reasonable French as well, because if you don't then your dream is unlikely to prove as pleasurable, or as successful, as you expect and you will certainly miss out on much of the enjoyment of French life.

In the following chapters I shall take you through some of the steps along the way of making your particular dream of life in *La Belle France* come true, pointing out some of the snags and drawbacks as well as the benefits and pleasures of having a home across the Channel.

CHAPTER TWO

MAKING THE DECISION

Why? Every dream has an underlying reason and so your dream of a home in France will have some main *raison d'être*. Perhaps you are approaching retirement and fancy releasing some capital by taking advantage of the lower cost of property in France; maybe you fancy a grander house than you could afford in Britain (and these can be bought for remarkably modest sums, though in questionable states of repair).

It may be that you fancy taking early retirement from a career in Britain and hope to supplement your pension by running a *pension* as it were and taking in guests while enjoying the better weather, the gentler pace of life and all the other features of life in France. I should have said rural France because one must never forget that in the cities, life across the Channel can be just as frenetic and stressful as in any British city or large town. Unless your dream is one of exchanging one rat race for another forget the idea of moving to a city unless you have to for career or business reasons.

A main reason for many dreams can be the better weather supposedly enjoyed by the French, but here it is worth doing a little research. Certainly there is better weather to be found in the right places, but would you tire of continual blistering sunshine? Could you afford to run the air conditioning day and night? Would you find yourself longing for a refreshing shower of rain or a dip in the sea? Much of France is a long way from the seaside although there are numerous inland resorts with river or pool bathing.

If wine is your pleasure then one need say little more: the district of a favourite *appellation* will have obvious appeal. But if you are contemplating doing more than drinking the nectar and have a desire to buy a vineyard, as many people have done quite successfully, then there is certainly no more typical a dream, and equally no bigger a set of potential problems for the uninitiated. Viticulture is a specialist business with high risks and high dependence on factors quite out of your control.

France has a population of roughly the same as the British Isles but a land area of about double the size so there is less of a feeling of crowds which results in easier parking, quieter roads and traffic and generally more space, especially in the country. The roads are better maintained than in Britain — they get less use after all — and fall into four categories. There are the *autoroutes à péage*. These are a network of toll motorways, two-lane for the most part and usually in parallel with an RN or other non-toll route. The tolls, very roughly, cost about as much as the petrol for a given distance and very conveniently can be paid for by credit card such as Visa, Access, Amex, etc. Payment is usually made at the end of the journey when you leave the *autoroute*. The speed limit is usually 130 kph and beware the trap which compares entry and exit times on your ticket to calculate your average speed. A sneaky trick you may say, but it is done! The service areas are mostly pleasant and well equipped and nearly all have a picnic area with tables and benches for picnics as well as a restaurant and the usual facilities. The loos may well be *à la Turque* style (hole in the ground!) but they will be clean and pleasant. If taken short on the road do as the French do and use the roadside!

Next down the hierarchy of the roads are the free Autoroutes or *Routes Nationale* to Autoroute standard. Marked on maps as RN they are maintained by the state and so preserve their identity throughout their length. They are for the most part excellent; frequently dead straight and undulating over the countryside. They have a normal speed limit of 110 kph.

Non-dual carriageway *Routes Nationale* are also state-maintained and similarly numbered to the dual carriageways.

Finally, the country is covered by a network of D roads. The D stands for *départementale*, implying that they are maintained by the *département* rather than the state. For this reason their numbering system can be confusing because each authority identifies its roads according to its own system and so it is thus normal for roads to change their number at departmental boundaries. These roads can be quite excellent, often dead straight for mile upon mile and carrying light traffic so it can be hard to observe the speed limit of 90 kph but beware the radar speed trap. Possession of a radar detector is illegal and the best warning is often the headlight flashes of oncoming traffic which will alert you to the trap ahead of you. If caught the motorist can expect an on-the-spot fine of as much as £250; and don't argue with the police. Remember, too, that speed limits are automatically reduced by 20 kph in inclement weather conditions.

Motoring in France can bring back to mind the way it was in the UK in the 1950s. The older reader will recall the advertisements which depicted the view of a straight road disappearing into the distance between rows of lombardy poplars above a long and aristocratic bonnet with the caption 'For the sheer joy of driving I would like to go there in an Alvis'. Some of that pleasure is still to be found on the D roads of France.

For the ardent DIY enthusiast France offers marvellous opportunities to buy cheap ruins and do them up. Planning rules are far more relaxed than we are used to and frequently it is only the local *maire* who has to be persuaded of the merit of your plans. Having work done professionally can run away with money, although the quality of the work will usually be excellent. Always get an estimate — *un devis* — and remember that French construction methods are sometimes radically different to those we are used to, with the result that some jobs can turn out to be infinitely harder to do to a French house than one in the UK. The dream can turn sour when the money runs out and the job is only half done and we must never forget that it is an offence to bounce a cheque in France. One can be banned from holding a bank account or worse, and life can become very difficult if money is a problem. It is true to say that more dreams of life in France have foundered on financial shoals than for any other reason. See Chapter 9.

What? The question of what to buy is bound up in that of why you are buying in the first place. The range of property on offer is vast, ranging from *châteaux* to run-down *fermettes*

— smallholdings — at prices to match. Every region has its own distinctive style of vernacular building — from the solid granite houses of Brittany to the low pitched roofs of Provence or the half-timbering of Normandy. Between the grandeur of the château and the semi-squalor of an old farmhouse are many very attractive and elegant houses called *maisons de maître*. It was one such which very nearly caused our downfall when we fell in love with it, or more accurately with its setting. Right beside the river Sarthe which is a large waterway and fully navigable, it satisfied my pretensions to grandeur perfectly and was a snip at FF 750,000. With visions of summers in the sun, memorable games of *boules* on the village concourse which was just outside the house and of sipping the *vin du pays* while cooking marvellous garlic-laced meals, we said we would have it within minutes of first seeing it. Next day, after a night of perfect sleep in feather beds smelling sweetly of lavender, we returned to measure up for curtains and carpets while the notary got on with things and drew up the contract of sale — *compromis de vente* — see Chapter 3. It was only then that we discovered that the only flushing loo was in an eight-family, three-holer outside, and further investigation showed that it would be a very difficult job, because of a peculiarity of French building methods, to bring the drains inside to where one would have wanted them. We also found that the house was riddled with rising damp and had an electricity system which must have been installed in the days of Michael Faraday.

We backed out of the purchase, causing the agent's pipe to go into wheeze overdrive as he sucked on it while hearing our decision. But we were saved in the nick of time, because once the contract of sale is signed, that is it and there can be no backing out by either party as is explained in more detail later.

Whatever you intend to buy, it is worth finding out a little about the type of property you have in mind because, unlike in the UK, there is no army of professional surveyors waiting to be instructed to examine and report on its structural condition. By and large the buyer is expected to make up his own mind as to the soundness of a property and, by the same token, the French are far less paranoid than the British when it comes to the odd patch of rising damp, or crack in a wall or woodworm in the roof timbers. 'The house has stood for 200 years; it won't fall down next week'. The attitude seems to be one of near total neglect until desperate measures and a virtually complete rebuild are needed. This applies particularly to public monuments and shrines which are allowed to decay almost to the point of collapse and are then rescued, in the nick of time, by a vast injection of cash. Just make sure that you are buying well short of the vast-injection-of-cash phase, unless that is your object and the doing up is expected to yield some profit as well as pleasure.

It is only by exploring on the ground that you will get a feel for the market, but there are several magazines which cater for the intending expatriate buyer. They will be advertised in the quality Sunday papers or can be obtained by or through some of the British agents who specialize in French property. Armed with these and a selection of maps you can start to plan your purchase campaign and get a feel for the relative values in different parts of the country and of different sorts of property. Some of the agents specializing in French property are listed on page 103.

It is also worth giving some serious consideration to the question of whether or not to buy some land with your property. The French are usually keen to own a bit of land with even the smallest house or cottage, and houses without any associated land or garden can be found at very cheap prices. Before rejecting such a deal ask yourself how often you intend to visit your French home. If the answer is infrequently, or for short periods, it may be an advantage to be spared the haymaking or silage-cropping every time you visit. There is no bigger dampener on a holiday than spending the first week of your precious fortnight hacking down the primeval jungle which has taken over since your last visit and is blowing weed seeds all over your neighbour's pristine plot. Our house has no garden whatsoever but we do have a strip of land between us and the river, which is owned by the commune. We cultivate it and have planted it up with roses etc., but there is no obligation on us to do so, though I suspect that if we were to stop looking after it there would be many villagers who would ask why. On the other hand an area of land may be fundamental to your needs and, if so, then obviously it must be acquired, together with all that its ownership entails. The question of where to buy will largely answer itself if one has properly addressed the questions of Why? and What? There is clearly no prospect of buying a smallholding to restore in the suburbs of Paris or a *Provençal mas* in the wilds of Brittany.

A major consideration is that of travel from and to the UK. If you plan to make frequent short visits then it makes sense to buy somewhere reasonably close to a Channel port or the Tunnel terminus, unless you can afford to fly. We always cross by ferry overnight at the western end of the Channel and so start our drive in France refreshed and alert. This means we can be home by lunch after having covered some 225 miles or so. A longer day's drive could see one in the Charente or Dordogne without too much strain, and with someone to share the driving even the Riviera is within reach. It all depends on personal preference, and the equation for you will depend on your enjoyment of driving, the proximity of your UK base to a port, and of its French counterpart's nearness to motorways or other good roads.

When doing your research the first thing you will need is a good set of maps of France, at least of your chosen target area. Probably the best all-round coverage is that provided by the *Michelin Yellow Series* to a scale of 1/2,000,000 or 1 cm = 2 km. These are readily available in bookshops and come in two sizes of sheet. The sheets 51–86 are smaller and each covers a lesser area than the sheets 230–245 and so they are easier to handle in a car, but the latter can make long-distance route planning easier by presenting a greater area on one sheet. The choice is yours. Once you have settled on a definite small area then it is time to invest in an IGN — *Institut Geographique National* — roughly the equivalent of the Ordnance Survey sheet in their *Séries Vertes*. These are to a scale of 1/100,000 or 1 cm = 1 km which is almost as detailed as our 1 inch = 1 mile maps, and again they can be bought in the UK. I well remember our own first house-hunting trips when we had failed to invest in any maps which identified the navigable rivers and canals. We had relied on the estate agents, who provided us with details of some houses to view, to have done their homework and to have met our specific requirement. It was therefore disappointing to find that an otherwise perfect house was beside a stream crossed by stepping stones and only navigable with difficulty even by ducks.

If the rivers and canals are of interest then another map to buy is that available from Imray Lorie Norie and Wilson, either on its own or as part of their *Guide to the Inland Waterways* of France (ISBN 0852880820). This book by David Edwards May is an invaluable mine of information on the rivers and canals, and in even greater detail are the *Carte Guide Navigation Fluviale* series published by *Editions Grafocarte* and obtainable from good yacht chandlers such as Captain O.M. Watts (ISBN 2904985107). These cover, in great detail, the rivers and canals of selected regions and are indispensable if you contemplate using the very extensive waterway network of France.

Among the general guides to France a particularly useful and informative one is the *AA Hachette Guide* (ISBN 0861457331). This contains cultural and historical information presented region by region, together with details of selected hotels, restaurants and places of interest. It can be a bit hard to follow unless you know the names of the larger towns in the region you are interested in but is a mine of information.

I mentioned air travel to France but it will be as well to do some research before committing yourself to an area on the expectation of being able to travel anywhere by air. There are comparatively few airports served direct from the UK: Beauvais, Paris, Rennes and Nantes in the north, Bordeaux in the west and Nice in the south have regular flights from Heathrow or Gatwick, but the many smaller regional airports can only be reached by changing at Paris. The picture changes daily so check with a travel agent and don't forget the expense of flying.

If you don't wish to drive each time then there is always the railway as an alternative. A glance at the TGV network may suggest possible areas for residence and, with the opening of the Tunnel, it is easier than ever before to make a train journey to your French hideaway, get the 2CV out of mothballs and be supping the local *vin du pays* before your friends have got home on the six-fifteen from Cannon Street. The ordinary SNCF network is extensive and has connections to the TGV system at various stations.

An important factor is of course the weather. As a simple generalization the weather gets hotter and drier the further south you go but there are particular areas which have their own micro climate. The Alps are obviously a special case, and remember that it is possible to ski all the year round in some of the higher resorts such as Tignes. An off-season timeshare flat in Tignes can be extremely cheap and if you are prepared to forgo much of the *après-ski* ambience then the skiing can be superb and memorable, especially if followed by windsurfing on the lake or a gentle walk looking for wild flowers in bright and warm sunshine.

Obviously the question of price will influence that of location and vice versa. The Channel coast will be more expensive than, say, 100 miles south, and the immediate surrounds of the ports even more so. Most of the desirable smallholdings for restoration will have been snapped up around Calais and Boulogne, but they can still be found reasonably close to Caen or Roscoff, in Normandy and Brittany respectively.

Those contemplating the purchase of their own vineyard will doubtless have ideas of varying degrees as to where they intend to settle, but it will be as well to try to contact other expatriates already in an area before committing yourself to the purchase of a property, no matter how desirable it may seem at first sight. Check out such matters as the status of the *appellation*. Can you sell your grapes to the local co-operative if you fail to gain *appellation contrôlée* status? Do the *chais* conform to modern standards or are you going to be faced with an enormous bill to replace all those lovely romantic-looking huge oak barrels with *inox* (stainless steel)? How old are the vines, and of what variety? Above all, what is the attitude of the locals to incomers? If bloody-minded they can make life very difficult as well as taking you to the proverbial cleaners financially. Only someone you trust who is on the ground can give you honest answers to some of these fundamental questions. It goes without saying that unless your colloquial French is reasonably good it is foolhardy in the extreme to try to enter commerce in any shape or form. Learn the *patois* first is a golden rule.

While the proximity of some of your fellow British can be a comfort and a support or help in some circumstances, there will be others when you will eschew it for all you are worth. Some areas are virtually overrun with *les Anglais*, and there is a danger that they will destroy that which attracted you to the place in the first instance if you add to their numbers. The Dordogne comes to mind as such an area, with Provence similarly afflicted by an influx of long-term expatriates and seasonal visitors of various nationalities. In other areas, by comparison, you may be part of a very small band and so acquire some sort of novelty value. Our house is in a region not well known by other British. It tends to be by-passed or driven through on the way to somewhere else, and so we enjoy the feeling of being a bit special. The villagers go out of their way to be helpful and welcoming and we have made firm friends with many of them, in a way which would not be possible if we were part of a mini invasion. Question your reasons for wanting to live in France and, if the answer has anything at all to do with enjoying *La Vie Française*, I suggest that you choose an area not noted for its popularity with other expatriates or tourists. Heaven knows, there are plenty of beautiful little bits of France which are totally undiscovered and unspoilt, where the shops all shut for two hours at lunchtime, the bread is baked freshly twice a day, the village *gendarme* takes his *pastis* under the shade of an umbrella in the square outside the bar at lunchtime, *boules* is played in the main street and the only cricket you will hear is the one chirruping in the sunshine in the branches of an old olive tree.

CHAPTER THREE

THE PROCESS OF BUYING

You know why you want it, what you want and where, so now it's time to start looking in earnest. The first thing to decide is whether or not you are going to enlist the help of a British estate agent with French connections. Unless your French is particularly good and you are prepared to spend a lot of time across the water this is a recommended course of action and a list of some firms offering this service is provided at the end of the book. You can also get hold of some names from the advertisements in the Sunday papers or in *France Magazine*, while *Country Life* has adverts for some of the more prestigious properties in its pages and especially in their occasional French issue. There are also some compilations of properties for sale produced in France and obtainable through some of the UK agents — these too are advertised in the Sunday papers and they will give you something to dream over by the fire during the winter since they include photos. It can be tremendous fun to visualize the property in its setting from the description in such a compilation and this is when the maps of the area come in handy. It's surprising just how much information can be gleaned from the *séries vertes* concerning the view and the general lie of the land.

Eventually the day comes when it is time to cross the Channel and get down to some serious looking. Immediately you will find a difference between the British and the French ways of selling property. The French have far fewer dedicated estate agents — *agents immobiliers* — than we do, because the notaries, who must by law handle the conveyancing, also tend to act as agents as well, rather as they do in Scotland. It is unusual to find more than one, or exceptionally two, agents in a town. They may go under the name of *Cabinet* .... or *Agence de* .... but the profession will be plain from the window and will be listed in *Yellow Pages* — *Pages Jaunes*. Notaries' offices are readily identifiable by the gilded oval sign exhibited over the door and they too will have details of properties for sale displayed on a board or in the window.

Whether it is an agent or a notary who is dealing with you over a particular property initially, it will always be a notary who will draw up the legal documents and contracts of sale and transfer. The agent is unlikely to have any printed details or glossy handouts but he or a member of his staff will accompany you on an inspection visit to any property in which you are interested. He will have a few basic details of all his properties in an illustrated file which you will be invited to browse through in his office and some will be displayed in the window as bait but it is expected that you will visit any which interest you. A British contact can cut through some of this delay by selecting likely prospects for you, but at the end of the day you will find yourself dashing about looking at your selection on the ground. If your target area is very specific, it can also be worthwhile to cruise around in the car looking for 'For Sale' — *à vendre* — signs. These will show you what is available as well as giving you the names of local agents and notaries.

You may come across the expression *à restaurer* — for restoration. This can cover anything from a tumbledown ruin to something needing no more than a new bathroom and kitchen. During our search we were asked by our agent of the day if we would be prepared to consider a property *à restaurer* and, fancying myself as a bit of a DIY expert, *'Bien sûr'*, I replied, expecting to find the place needing a little plastering, perhaps some replumbing and rewiring and maybe some work on the roof. The agent led us at a furious pace up hill and down dale through fords and farmyards scattering geese and ducks in the wind of our passing and eventually we dropped down a steep lane between high banks bedecked with primroses and cowslips to a derelict mill beside the Mayenne. It was in an idyllic situation with breathtaking views up and downstream from its position on the island between the weir and the lock. A silver torrent of water cascaded over the sole remaining lock gate and a flock of pigeons took wing at our approach, but the phrase *à restaurer* took on a whole new meaning. The roof and the internal floors had all collapsed to ground-floor level where they lay on the rotting remains of the wheel and the mill machinery; there wasn't a single window frame in place and any work on the outside of the building would have necessitated the building of scaffolding up from the river bed. For a few moments we dreamed of throwing up my career in England and of becoming French property restorers but in the sober light of our bank balance we realized that the work needed to save this beautiful building was way beyond my capabilities and our means. The look of disappointment on the agent's face as we said, *'Non, merci'* had to be seen to be believed. If your dream is of doing just what we decided not to, then be brave but be prepared for anything. There are literally dozens of derelict mills along the rivers of France, all waiting for someone to turn them into superb residences. Some are viable propositions and some most definitely are not unless you have a bottomless pit of money to draw on. But do look at some of them. Equally the countryside is littered with semi-derelict farm buildings going to rack and ruin and capable, most of them, of becoming charming residences given a little imagination and the attention of a dreamer (plus a certain amount of cash and/or hard work).

While looking, it is as well to spend a week or so at a time staying in an hotel or bed and breakfast — *Chambre d'Hôte*. There are plenty of guides to help you and I particularly recommend the *Logis de France* chain where the establishments are graded and given chimney ratings along the line of RAC stars. The French Government Tourist Office in London will send you as many lists as you want. Since you probably know roughly where you want to look and, hence where to stay for the search, it is also worth writing in advance to the Chamber of Commerce — *Syndicat d'Initiative* — at the *Mairie* of the biggest local town to ask for the names of solicitors and agents as well as for a list of local *Chambres d'Hôtes* and *Gîtes*. Staying at either of these can be a useful introduction to the neighbourhood in which you may be settling and you could pick up some useful snippets of information from your host or hostess. *Chambres d'Hôtes* can be exceptionally good value and are an excellent way of meeting the people and practising your French, while *Gîtes* give you more independence to come and go as and when you want. If you have it in mind to enter the letting business yourself, then what better way could there be to see how it is done and what the opposition will be!

Eventually, one sunny day when the grasshoppers are chirruping away and the scent of thyme is on the air, your dream house will turn up — be it a mini chateau or a small-holding or a modest little fisherman's cottage beside the sea in Brittany.

Now is the time to make sure it is really what you want and to discover any hidden snags. Ask about the local taxes (see Chapter 6), the cost of water and the reliability of the supply in summer if it is from a private source. Ask if the house is on main drains — *eaux usées assainissement* — or does it have its own septic tank — *fosse septique* — as is common in the countryside? Is the electrical installation in good order, the roof sound (by French standards) and are the boundaries clearly defined and marked? Don't go looking for a mains gas connection because they are virtually unknown in France, except in some of the larger towns. Gas is a popular fuel but is usually supplied in bottles and these can be exchanged at most garages. There are several suppliers and each tends to have its own unique fitting system, so you can't swap between suppliers.

This catechism of things to check is necessary because, generally, it is unusual to employ a surveyor to conduct a structural survey on most houses. They exist and are called *geomètre* because their prime purpose is the surveying of land to establish just where the boundaries lie (often during disputes which seem to be a preoccupation of the French). Chapter 7 will tell you about some of the peculiarities of French construction methods so don't give up because you have to back your own judgement. There is a particular thrill in proving your judgement right and seeing your dream materialize as you set about getting your house to your liking.

Once you have decided on a particular property it is over to the notary, either the one who has shown you the house in the first place or one appointed by the vendor or his agent or chosen by you, because only a notary can handle the legal formalities of sale and transfer. As the buyer you have the right to select the notary or even to appoint your own to act in concert with the vendor's. As a foreigner it is unlikely that you will wish to dispute the selection made by the vendor and the way in which a notary works means that he has to protect the interests of both parties to a transaction. If you have been dealing with an agent it is advisable that he should have been a member of their professional body FNAIM and essential that he have on display in his office a certificate giving the number of his professional charter and the amount of his guarantee, which must be for at least FF 500,000, together with the names and details of his guarantors. Without these he is not authorized to receive deposits or to handle money on behalf of his clients (and really isn't worth bothering with). The same information must, by law, be printed on all his official stationery. The agent may be acting as sole agent under a *mandat exclusif* or he may be one of several agents instructed under a *mandat simple* in which latter case the vendor reserves the right to negotiate with purchasers himself. In either case it is illegal to try to cut the agent out after he has shown you a property — he is guaranteed his fee, and it is usually the purchaser who pays it!

As to price, if you are working to a tight budget always remember that the asking price — *prix demandée* — will be bumped up by sometimes as much as 15% to cover the fees of the agent and/or the notary, both of which are payable by the purchaser, together with a number of taxes and registration fees. There is little to be saved by buying through a notary — he claims an agency fee as well as his conveyancing fees.

You may see prices quoted as *frais compris* which literally means fees included — enquire which fees are covered by this offer before doing your sums. The expressions *hors frais* or *hors taxes* means that fees or taxes have not been included. Taxes such as Capital Gains Tax on the sale may be payable by the vendor (see Chapter 9), and it is the notary who is responsible for collecting them and passing them to the appropriate ministry. The notary acts for both parties in the conveyance. He proves title, conducts searches, etc., and is accountable for the efficient conduct of his work to the Ministry of Justice by whom he is appointed and licensed. In a complicated transaction, or if you fear that there might be some skulduggery in a particularly close-knit community, it might be advisable to employ your own notary to safeguard your interests. In this case the two notaries will share the same fee (which is calculated on a sliding scale according to the price of the property), as would have been payable to the single notary so it doesn't cost you any more to have this added protection. A set of these scales and the other taxes and fees can be found at the end of this book.

The first step taken by the notary is the preparation of the contract of sale — *compromis de vente*. This is usually a preprinted proforma document and, of course, in French, but there are bilingual versions available and, if you are using a British firm to help you, they ought to have them and will persuade the notary to accept their use. The *compromis de vente* is a binding contract on both parties and its signing is accompanied by the payment of a deposit of usually 10% of the price agreed. Your property may have been offered at a *prix à discuter* meaning 'for negotiation'. The contract of sale will record the agreed price.

If you need a mortgage to complete the purchase, it is essential to declare the fact and have it recorded in the contract because failure to obtain your funding within a certain time is just about the only legally acceptable excuse for failure to complete the purchase. If you fail to complete for any other reason your deposit will be forfeited and given to the vendor. If the vendor fails to honour his contract he can be forced to pay you twice the deposit sum. You cannot be gazumped and neither can you try to beat down the price once it has been agreed.

Six weeks or so after signing the contract, the notary will have the final document — *acte finale* — ready for signature. This is when your wallet takes the strain as you cough up the remaining part of the price as well as the fees, and the sale is completed, so be sure that you have the money available and ready. A great many dreams have foundered because purchasers have been seduced into signing a contract before they have disposed of the property in Britain which is to fund their purchase. You can't stall the transaction in the same way as in the UK and chains are virtually unknown.

The notary will register the transfer at the Land Registry and the deeds will be available a couple of weeks later. If you cannot be present for the signing and transfer of the *acte finale* it is possible to give power of attorney to somebody to do it for you — this again is where a UK agent can be a great help if he has a representative in France who is thoroughly familiar with the procedures.

Even at the very first stage of the purchase it is essential to give some consideration to the ultimate disposal of the property on the death of you or your spouse if married. Chapter 11 deals with the subject of wills and one way of mitigating the effects of the *Code Napoléon* is to buy your house *en tontine*. Ask your notary for his advice once you are clear in your own mind what you wish to happen in the event of your eventual or untimely death, but don't put it off because, as set out in Chapter 15, the results can be most distressing for your successors if your will is found to be wanting or non-existent.

The notary should notify all the interested parties such as local authorities and utility suppliers of the change of ownership but it is as well to drop in at the local *Mairie* — which is the administrative centre — and make yourself known. Local government is far more 'local' in France than in the UK and the mayor is an important and respected figure in his community. It is especially important to have him on your side if you are planning an extension or major alterations to your dream house.

If you are buying a new house or one being built, there are a few little quirks which are as well to know. Before settling on a particular plot it is essential to consult the town planning charter — *Certificat d'Urbanisme* — at the local *Hôtel de Ville* or *Mairie*. This details the type of permitted development on any particular area of land and the building density. Also consult the Plan of Land Occupancy in the Departmental Office of Supply in the principal town of the *département*, which will identify which areas of land have been designated for development and what municipal services are expected to be installed. You may find that the local authority is buying up the plots for resale in order to deter speculation and price escalation by individuals. In choosing a plot the same principles apply as anywhere else — is it facing the right way, is the area liable to flooding or subsidence, is there a reliable water supply if no mains is available, where can you reasonably site a septic tank if there are no main drains, can you gain access easily from a road, is the plot reasonably level or will it require a JCB to work on it for a week or so before you can start to dig the footings, etc., etc.?

Finally, whilst you may have considerable freedom as to what you build, there are still certain building regulations to observe — *les servitudes* — and the town planning charter will specify any restrictions on height or style. By and large you will be expected to conform to the local style and most builders will have a selection of plans for you to choose from, rather like the choice of styles on any modern estate in the UK. Do be particular about rights of way for both passage of people and animals and also for such things as water pipes over or under your land. It is in this exercise that it is probably wise to retain the services of a *geomètre*.

The dreaded planning permission is present across the Channel and is called *permis de construire*. It is required before building any new house or extending an existing one. Your application must specify all the usual relevant details of who you are and what you wish to do, supported by plans and drawings which must include details of the sanitary installation. You also have to include details of any demolition which will be involved and request permission for it. You will have to submit the application to the local council by hand or by registered post and get a receipt for it. Expect to wait about two months for the permission to be granted unless there are any snags. If the proposed building is of less than 170 square metres floor area you are allowed to assemble the application yourself, but if it exceeds this size you have to employ an architect and so it is logical to have him make the application as well.

Most regions offer a free architectural service which will help you to stay within their building guidelines. Do not be put off — there is probably a lot more freedom to do your own thing than you expect, and you can indulge your whims fairly freely, unless they are extreme.

Many villages have small areas of development owned by

the local authority and with plots for sale with services installed. Ask at the local *Mairie* if this route to acquisition appeals to you.

The formalities of engaging a builder to put your dream house together are not too different to those in the UK. Make sure that there are no loopholes in any clauses in the contract where it specifies cost, estimates or final price to be paid as well as the timetable for building and stage payments. Whatever else you do, do take advice from the appropriate professional even if your French is superb.

Altogether, complicated though it may sound, the procedure is remarkably straightforward in the vast majority of cases, and certainly a lot simpler than in Britain. It is also considerably quicker. If buying an existing house the contract can be prepared within a couple of days and the completion follows just six weeks later — then your dream is yours.

CHAPTER FOUR

RENTING PROPERTY

It may be that you decide to defer buying a house until you have had some time to look around. It may be more convenient to rent first. If you do so you will be in good company because the majority of the French still live in rented accommodation, but there are some points to be aware of.

The first thing to learn is that very little property in France is let furnished except for holidays or as secondary residences. Virtually all long-term leases are for unfurnished premises, and this is probably what you will want and be offered by any agent you approach.

If, however, you do rent furnished then be aware first of all that there is no obligation on the part of the landlord to provide you with a written lease agreement. It is in your own interests to try and get one and it ought to specify, among other things, how the local taxes — *Taxe foncière* and *Taxe d'habitation* (see Chapter 6) — are to be apportioned between you. If you can't get this sorted out beware of the whole situation and look elsewhere. The tenancy should run for an agreed fixed period at the end of which it terminates, but if you fail to pay the rent it will lapse automatically. If the landlord allows you to stay in residence after the end of the tenancy then you acquire the right to reasonable notice if he decides to terminate it subsequently. What constitutes reasonable in this context can vary from place to place, so take advice if entering this area of tenancy. There is no regulation of rents — they are set entirely by market forces. If, as is strongly advised, you get a written agreement make sure that it includes a statement of the condition of the property and contents — *état des lieux* — or else be prepared to be invited to pay for the redecoration and refurnishing of the entire place at the end of the tenancy. Also have the deposit amount recorded: my son lost a FF 8,000 deposit to a landlord in Juan-les-Pins for lack of a written agreement for a flat he rented for two years.

An unfurnished lease is bound by the provisions of a law passed in 1989 which amended earlier legislation. Briefly it requires that there be a written lease agreement document which, however, does not have to be drawn up by a solicitor. It must specify the relevant dates of start, and finish (if agreed), the rent and the review period (which cannot be less than a year, and reviews are to be linked to the cost of the construction index). Also to be included are the frequency of payment of rent and the details of the deposit. The deposit may be as much as two months' rent, provided that the landlord is not asking also for more than two months rent in advance. The tenant has the right to insist on being given a receipt for his rent and on monthly payment intervals, in which case the landlord can then demand a deposit which he has to return within two months of the termination of the lease after deducting any sums due to him as of right.

The tenant may be obliged to insure the property — check up on your liability but be advised that the landlord cannot specify with whom you effect the insurance. The rest of the agreement should contain the usual and expected clauses concerning peaceable enjoyment of the property by the tenant and any other residents with whom he shares facilities, e.g. stairs in a block of flats. Most important, as with the furnished letting, is the statement of condition as it will protect you in the case of a dispute at the end of your stay.

Flats can be a nightmare for landlord and tenant if things go wrong with parts of the building which affect more than one occupier. A typical example is the leaking roof and, in this sort of situation, one is well advised to consult a solicitor for advice before agreeing to any solution proposed by your landlord whose sole interest will be himself and his own peaceable existence.

Basically the property-renting scene is no less and no more the province of sharks than in Britain. Where they exist is in the expected areas of the Côte d'Azur and Paris, and the best advice one can be given is to ask lots of questions and never to rent without a proper written agreement, whether legally required or not. In the country there are many superb properties available to rent and where you can reside while seeking your dream house. In this way you can make doubly sure that the area is what you expected it to be.

It may even be worth considering renting your French home permanently. Unless you are seeking a place in one of the more popular seaside resorts it could prove as cheap and will save you all the fuss involved in ownership as well as avoiding tying up a lump of your capital. In some of the remote inland areas which are so quintessentially French, property to rent can be remarkably reasonable.

CHAPTER FIVE

SETTING UP AND SETTLING IN

Furnishing the house is an exercise which soon shows you the differences in costs between Britain and France. Generally new furniture in France is considerably more expensive than we are used to. There are several chains akin to MFI — and *Monsieur Meuble* come to mind — but it can save a lot of money to buy second hand from a *brocante*. (The term *brocante* covers anything from antiques to house clearance items but a *brocante* is the most likely source of reasonable furniture.) If buying from a *brocante* or a house clearance dealer be prepared to douse everything in Rentokil.

One advantage of buying new from the larger chains is their van hire facility. For a modest sum, or even free for the first couple of hours, they will hire you a self-drive van — *camionnette*. You provide your own Yorkie bars, dress the part and join in the fray of driving a vehicle in which your unfamiliarity with driving to the right is no longer obvious from your GB plate. You can, of course, use the van to pick up some bits and pieces from the second-hand shop as you go past. The larger DIY stores offer a similar service to transport the bricks, plaster, sand and all the rest of your purchases home. The French for delivery is *livraison* — stores not offering a van for hire will probably offer delivery for a fee or even free, within a certain range.

If you are furnishing from scratch, it can be worthwhile to ship a load out from England. A look at *Yellow Pages* or through *France Magazine* will give you the names of carriers specializing in full or part loads to France, and if you can wait a few weeks until the owner has a trip planned it can be modestly priced and an overall saving over purchasing in France. With the exception of the beds, the cooker and fridge which we bought in France (white goods are dearer than we are used to and are mostly of home manufacture because the French do not allow the same scale of imports from Japan) we furnished our house almost completely from car-boot sales in Britain (which don't seem to have caught on in France yet) and our own attic, taking the stuff out bit by bit in my boat which we trailed out every summer. In theory any goods and chattels imported for furnishing a holiday house in which you do not intend to live permanently need to be declared to Customs on import into the country. It will help your cause to get them in without the imposition of any duty or tax if they are clearly used and not brand new. In practice if you don't take too much at a time it is perfectly feasible to take the stuff in bit by bit. We took out all our booty in this way and on one occasion I put so much stuff in the boat that the mudguards on her trailer were rubbing on the wheels so I had to jack her up and take the mudguards off before she would move! Not recommended. Much of the weight was paint which is fearfully expensive in France as well as being generally of inferior quality.

Electrical voltages are the same, although you will have to change the plugs on any appliances previously used in the UK. If you are in a hurry to equip the house for living then a visit to the nearest *Leclerc, STOC* or *Super U* supermarket will provide virtually everything you need if you can't wait to visit the nearest street market, but be prepared to pay maybe as much as 25 to 50% extra for domestic electrical appliances — *électro ménager*. There also seems to be more pleasure in shopping in France — maybe it is because the assistants are pleasant and well mannered as well as being genuinely helpful.

Our dream started with us eating out of doors in the sunshine off a plastic patio table, sleeping on campbeds and cooking on a camping gas stove until things came together. With the fine weather and the novelty of everything it was fun — it was part of the dream. When it got too hot we jumped into the river for a swim.

Remember, too, that most French houses have shutters on the windows so it is quite possible to do without curtains until you have rummaged through your own stock of window hangings from previous houses and which somehow never seem to fit the windows of the next house. As you would expect, the windows open inwards and frequently are on lift-off or knock-out pin hinges so it is an easy job to remove them for painting as well as making cleaning them a simple task. Remember, when putting up rails, that you will need to be able to pull the curtains clear of the windows at the side so you can open them. Allow plenty of overhang and mount the rails high enough for the windows to open under them.

Reasonably priced furnishing fabrics are harder to find in the average French town and I haven't yet discovered an equivalent to Sue Foster for warehouse ends etc., though doubtless one exists. Wallpaper is plentiful but may not be to your taste. While not wishing to totally anglicize our house we did draw the line at the maroon flock wallpaper and settled for Laura Ashley instead.

Becoming accepted by the locals can take time, just as it can in parts of Britain, but there are ways to assist the process. First and foremost, no matter how poor your grammar and syntax or your accent, speak the language. Force yourself to talk to the assistant at the checkout and in your local bakers' shop — discuss the weather or the price of fish or anything but talk in French. Strike up a conversation with anyone who is prepared to spare the time for a chat and you will find that your halting speech will improve and they will appreciate your effort. It can also help to have some sort of novelty or to be unusual or eccentric in some way or other. We had our steam launch which was a great door-opener, as villagers came to hang over the river wall and look at her. I gave a few trips in her to locals and it helped us to get to know them. A classic or vintage car would have the same effect — a friend in the Dordogne has a Rolls-Royce Phantom II which causes heads to turn whenever it passes. If you are living in a small village which has managed to keep its shop, patronize it. Just as in the UK, the village shop is under great pressure and many are struggling to survive. They are the centre for gossip and it is worth using your local shop whenever you can. It is a perfect place in which to practise your French without feeling too self-conscious. Remember that it was probably part of the vision which first attracted you to the place in the first instance. By the same token it won't help your acceptance if you immediately set about knocking your house down and rebuilding it to resemble a Sussex cottage; once again remember the dream and the things which attracted you to your particular hideaway. In certain parts too it can be very tricky to get involved in any sort of discussion of World War Two — memories run deep and local animosities can be stirred quite unwittingly. Many of the French are also deeply conscious of their debt to the English-speaking world, but that doesn't mean that they want to be constantly reminded of it, and some have come to resent their liberators. Local politics is best avoided until you are well established.

'But who looks after your house when you aren't there?' is one of the most commonly asked questions of the non-resident owner of a house in France. One suspects that the questioners have just read of the vandalism of yet another holiday cottage in Wales and are fearful that the same sort of anarchy prevails in France. Obviously the answer will vary from region to region, and my experience in a village in Maine-Anjou will not necessarily be repeated all over the country. I can honestly say that all we do is close the shutters, which lock from inside the house, turn off the water and drain the system before the winter and pull out all the fuses except the one for the dehumidifier, lock the house up and leave it. In five years the only problem has been a propensity for the local spiders to try to secure the door with their cobwebs, and a lavatory pan which froze and pushed the bottom out of the trap. Now I put salt in the traps when closing down in November and it stays there until March or April when the house is reawakened for the spring. There has been no vandalism whatsoever, and that despite the house not being overlooked, although it is passed daily by dozens of villagers walking their dogs or just out for a stroll in the evening. I deliberately haven't fitted a letterbox so as to deter any malevolent individuals from pushing unwanted objects through it and to prevent the house being filled with the handbills and leaflets with which the French seem to love advertising anything from the latest promotion at *Le Clerc* to a concert in the town or a visit by the mobile tool shop.

Probably the best security will come from friendship with

your neighbours; the curtains twitch in France no less than in Britain and neighbourhood watch has nothing on the observational capacity of a French neighbour. If living in a block of flats, the key to security is the *concièrge* — make friends with her or him and it will yield dividends far beyond the bottle of Scotch given as a Christmas box.

CHAPTER SIX

THE BILLS

'The sunshine will keep down the fuel bills — and we'll burn our own wood in any case' is part of the dream of many who settle in the more southerly areas of France and there is of course some truth in it. But there are more bills to be considered than just the fuel and any thoughts of living for next to nothing are bound to be dashed.

To start with, the council tax equivalent is two separate taxes. First of these is the *Taxe Foncière* which is levied on any building, whether occupied or not. For our little house it is just over FF 600 per year while the adjacent large garage and its loft, of greater total floor area than the house, is rated at FF 500 per year. The tax is paid to the local treasury — *tresor public* — in our case by the end of September for the year in question. The first tax is waived for two years on newly built or extensively restored properties.

The second local tax is *Taxe d'Habitation*. This is levied on habitable and furnished properties, whether occupied or not. In amount it is comparable to *Taxe Foncière* and, for our house in a largish village, is about FF 1,400 per year payable by the end of December. This tax is payable by whoever is the registered owner of a property on 1 January, even if he sells it before the tax is demanded. By completing our purchase in mid-January we saved ourselves our first year's tax, though unaware of it at the time. Some reductions are made to the retired or those who have an elderly relative living with them. Like *Taxe Foncière*, *Taxe d'Habitation* is paid to the local treasury and you may notice that even the forms used to render the demands are similar in layout and style. These forms identify the proportions of each tax which will be devoted to the region, the local urban centre and your own village or *commune*.

It can be dangerous to generalize when comparing taxes

across the Channel but it does seem to work out that the combined *Taxes Foncière* and *d'Habitation* bill works out to a total considerably less than council tax for an equivalent property in the UK and for much the same level of service. The total to be paid will, of course, depend greatly on the area in which you are living and on the political flavour of the local council. The local mayor's office will always be able to advise you on the level of charge for any particular property in which you are interested. Payment can be made in cash at the office, or the bill can be sent to your UK address and you can pay by Eurocheque if necessary.

France has no oil resources of her own and so petroleum products are expensive and the burning of oil, for central heating purposes, is uncommon; the French much prefer to burn bottled gas or wood, of which there is a greater abundance than north of the Channel. One of the status symbols of the rural areas is the log pile. Frequently the store of seasoning wood will dwarf the house or smallholding to which it belongs, as it is piled up in a Great Wall of China or lesser Hadrian's Wall around the property. Even flat dwellers who may not even have a fireplace in which to burn it will have a cord or two stacked up outside on the balcony, as if to say to the neighbours that they have an estate in the country and the wood is all from it. Buying wood, however, can be remarkably difficult until someone introduces you to someone else who knows of a man who sells a little wood from his backyard. Then you are in and can join the logocracy and build your own little Berlin Wall of wood, seasoning in the wind and rain. If living deep in the country, it is almost *de rigueur* to cover your pile with old plastic fertilizer bags or some such material. There is little serious risk of it being stolen because it is so bulky relative to its value. But do be careful to get it split or cut to the right length and size for your fire or stove before delivery — some woods toughen incredibly when they age and can be the very devil to split when seasoned; oak being one of them. If unused to burning wood, be advised that if you don't want to have problems with the tarring-up of your flues and chimney, the wood should be seasoned for a minimum of two years, and the best is much older than that.

Central heating oil is called *Mazout* and is supplied by tanker in just the same way as we are used to.

Electricity comes in much the same size and shape as we use in the UK, i.e. 220 volts AC and with three-phase supply available if you require more than the usual domestic power. There are several tariffs available and probably the most popular and practical one will be the two-tier system comparable to our old white-meter tariff. This has two charging rates, day — *heures pleines* — and night off-peak — *heures creuses*. The meter responds to a signal sent down the supply wires and moves from one set of counters to another. This signal can also close a relay so that certain devices only come on during off-peak time. Typically water heaters are so wired that they normally run on off-peak power but can be overridden to heat up during the day at standard rate in case you run out or arrive on holiday in the middle of the morning and want some hot water. The controls are also clever enough to automatically revert to off-peak next time the changeover signal is received. The changeover time can be something of a movable feast, depending on demand at the time.

Having a considerable nuclear capacity, the French are anxious to keep up their night base-load because it is difficult to shut down a nuclear plant for the night. At the time of writing the costs per kWh of electricity are FF 0.3287 off-peak and FF 0.5768 daytime rate. In addition there is a standing charge of FF 67.63 per month for a maximum demand of 6kW. If your property is large and has a greater maximum demand then the standing charge will be higher. There is also a local tax levied via your electricity bill at typically 0.5% and finally VAT — *TVA* — is payable at 5.5% on the standing charge and at 18.6% on both the consumption and the local tax.

Bills are rendered quarterly or six-monthly and if your meter cannot be read because of your absence, estimates, whereby you will feel that you are supplying the whole village, will be made. This happened to us and so we got in touch with EDF — *Electricité de France* — who are the nationalized supply company and asked them to shift our meter onto the outside wall where their inspector could read it. This was all fixed up by letter and the inspector came at exactly the appointed time and, for a modest charge, did exactly as I wanted. He also reversed the polarity of the wires to the fuse box which someone had got the wrong way round. The bills arrive in an intelligible form complete with tear-off return slip and they are quite prepared to send the bill to a British address and to accept payment by Eurocheque.

Gas costs varying amounts depending on how much you buy at a time. It is most commonly used for cooking and a 25 kg bottle refill costs around FF 90. Remember always to keep the receipt for a bottle in order to claim its deposit value back when exchanging it for a refill. The nationalized gas company — *Gaz de France* — is run alongside the electric company and they are frequently referred to together as EDF/GDF.

In my experience EDF/GDF is an efficient outfit which is almost a pleasure to deal with; their employees are courteous and polite and even try to clear up behind themselves.

Paraffin or kerosene for lamps is available in small five-litre containers at an exorbitant price. It goes by the fancy name of *pétrole desaromatisé*. Remember petrol is *essence*: paraffin is *pétrole*. In contrast, white spirit is remarkably cheap and so is meths. So if the wine begins to pall . . .

Water is supplied by various undertakings — in our case it comes from the quaint-sounding *Compagnie Fermière de Services Publics*. Water is metered and the charge, as in Britain, covers drainage if you are on main drains — *eaux usées/assainissement*. For a consumption of 22 m^3 the bill is typically FF 365. If you have your own drains leading to a septic tank reduce this by about 20% — it is the water which costs, not the sewerage.

For several years I resisted having the telephone installed as being contrary to our dream of utter peace away from it all. I also expected the standing charges to mirror those of BT and to be more than I was prepared to pay for occasional use. The growing frailty of near relatives, and the need for them to be able to contact us in emergency, eventually changed that and I made the pleasant discovery that French phone charges are more modest than those of BT. It cost about FF 300 to be connected from scratch, I bought the instrument (don't try to use a BT phone in France — it won't plug in) and the monthly standing charge is only about FF 45. Call charges are based on a unit charge of, currently, FF 0.73 which buys three minutes of local call up to about 40 km radius, 45 seconds out to 80 km and 19 seconds for greater distances in France. The phone system is no longer the standing joke it once was and is now thoroughly modern and up to date. Public phones are a mixture of card and cash devices. The former take cards which can be bought at most *Tabacs* and come in various values. They carry a small microchip and are not interchangeable with BT cards. Telephone numbers are almost always composed of an even number of digits and frequently, but not invariably, the first two are the *département* number. When quoting a number it is always given in a pair form. Thus 43921453 is written 43 92 14 53 and quoted as *quarante-trois, quatre-vingt-douze, quatorze, cinquante-trois*. Any other way of quoting a number will cause utter confusion, but it is not necessary to break the number up when dialling except sometimes to pause and wait for a renewed dialling tone between the pairs of an overseas dialling code. Directory enquiries is a service best avoided if possible, but it is relatively easy to get yourself connected to an English-speaking operator by dialling 19 00 44. Better still, if you are after a number in Britain, it is easier to ring up a friend in the UK and ask them to look up the number. When dialling a British STD code from abroad omit the first 0 when adding the code to the international code number (19 44).

Fax machines work similarly to those in Britain and one bought in Britain will work in France — until it breaks down. When this happens, expect its repair to be difficult at best and impossible at worst, unless it is a French manufactured machine, or one widely sold in France. If unfamiliar with a fax, it is a revelation how useful it can be when you have one.

A particular service available via the phone, throughout France, is *Minitel*. Briefly this is a computer link through which one can access information and also conduct transactions. For example it is possible to look up the times of trains and then to book and pay for tickets through the home *Minitel* terminal. Also available are weather forecasts, share-price information, theatre programmes and tickets and many many more services. It also acts as a computer billboard system and has been of great benefit to the organizers of strikes in France who communicated with one another via their *Minitels*. There are even *Minitel* house agents so you can find your next dream house via the service. Charges vary according to the service accessed and the duration of the access but typically are between FF 0.36 and FF 2.19 per minute. The cost of any access can be displayed both before and after the call has been made. The terminal is hired for about FF 85 per month.

Insurance against third-party risks is obligatory for the owner of any property and is commonly included in the standard buildings' insurance offered by companies on either side of the Channel. We use the brokers Europea of Horsham who have considerable experience of overseas insurance. If you wish to do it all in France, your house agent or notary will be able to advise you and may well be an agent for one or other of the larger companies. It is also prudent to insure your dream from the moment of signing the contract of sale, just as it is wise to insure properties in Britain from the exchange of contracts. It wouldn't be much fun to become the proud but uninsured owner of a smouldering ruin in the Auvergne, struck by lightning the night before the final document was signed. Despite this advice it is as well to be aware of a peculiarity of French insurance whereby insurance of a property automatically passes from a vendor to a purchaser and he is deemed to have taken over the policy and will be expected to give the requisite notice if he does not intend to continue with the company in question. If he fails to give this notice he may be chased for premiums. Ultimate responsibility for paying the premiums rests with the vendor until the policy is cancelled. It is important therefore that the contract of sale deals specifically with this point. The reputation of French insurance companies for wriggling off the hook is even worse than the British, and since French law does not require that even the mandatory third-party cover is taken out in France, my advice would be to use a British insurer whose policy you will perhaps be able to understand. In this context, however, make sure that the cover is written under British law and is not a French affair despite having been written in Britain. This can occur if you use an insurer who has offices in France.

The costs of running a car will depend on whether you do

it from Britain or transfer your vehicle to France permanently. If you do the latter, as will in any case become obligatory if you become a resident, it will be necessary to visit the *préfecture* of the area in which you are living and it will be a lot simpler if you have already owned and registered the car in Britain for at least six months and have paid British taxes on its purchase. The *préfecture* will probably want to see your passport, residence permit, the vehicle's registration document (V5) and form 857A obtained from Customs at the port of importation. You may also have to have it mechanically examined and a certificate issued by the inspectorate at the local *Service des Mines*. You will be issued with your French registration documents and tax sticker and will need to get your new number plates made up. Note that French number plates are reissued or renewed annually and that they identify the region of issue by the last two digits. There is no cradle-to-scrapyard identification, such as we are used to, which remains with the vehicle forever. If you change your residence while living in France it is necessary to re-register your car in the new location within three months of moving.

The inspection by the *Service des Mines* is more nit-picking than our MOT test and is being used to keep out bangers. The French have quite enough of these of their own and are becoming keen to promote sales of their own cars in order to help what has become a depressed and highly subsidy-dependent industry.

French insurance for cars follows the same pattern as in Britain with a bare minimum cover roughly equivalent to our Road Traffic Act cover being mandatory. If effected in France, this cover is considerably less than in Britain and excludes, for example, any cover of the driver, or of the car if it is not actually being driven by the insured. It is not covered if broken down, parked in the street or if you skid into another car. Comprehensive cover is considerably more expensive and so more motorists do without it and carry their own risk — hence the greater number of battered vehicles which you will see on the road. Even if you get a so-called comprehensive policy it will be so hedged about with exclusions and let-out clauses that you may wonder why you bothered.

No-claims bonuses can be earned but the opposite principle also applies as policies are loaded after claims have been made and comprehensive cover may be refused to anyone with a poor record or who has committed a traffic offence. It is better to try to insure your car from Britain if at all possible and as is now quite permissible under EEC law, though this may entail occasional return trips to the home country. If doing this for a car run and registered in France, be sure to get a certificate — *vignette d'assurance* — which will satisfy the French authorities when you fix it inside your windscreen, as required by French law.

Your motoring organization in the UK will be able to give detailed advice if you contemplate importing a car into France — and remember, too, that there is no direct equivalent to the AA or RAC in France so roadside assistance usually has to be got from passing motorists or the nearest garage, unless you have extended your cover to include the continent and have access to the service of *Europ Assistance* or some similar organization.

Buying a second-hand car in France exposes one to all the same risks as it does at home, so take care. Having selected the vehicle, do not drive it until you have insurance in your name for it. Registration will involve a visit to the *Prefecture* taking with you the certificate of sale (which is an official document issued by *préfectures* to vendors), the cancelled log book — *Carte Grise* — and your passport or residence permit and finally the *Autobilan* or test certificate which the vendor is obliged to have obtained by submitting the car for a *Contrôle Technique* test if it is more than five years old. The *préfecture* will confirm that there is no outstanding hire purchase agreement on the car, either from their own records if it was previously registered in the area or by reference to the old area of registry. You will also need to buy a *vignette* (roughly equivalent to our licence fee, but costing less and on a sliding scale according to horsepower and age with older cars paying less), from the local *perception*, unless a valid one is already on the car. The *vignette* is renewable annually in November and during that month can be obtained from your local *tabac*. The cost of a *vignette* also varies from one area to another. It is not identifiable as belonging to a particular car and so is clearly worth stealing for a couple of months until cars without one have all been rounded up by the police, so keep your car locked up during November and December. The *vignette* must be displayed inside your windscreen, together with the similar disc — *vignette d'assurance* — issued by your insurance company, at all times. You also get a receipt when buying your *vignette* — keep it in case the *vignette* is stolen because it will help you get another one without having to pay again. That done, enjoy the space of the French roads but remember that their accident rates are roughly double those in Britain.

CHAPTER SEVEN

DOING IT YOURSELF

Whether it is a deliberate part of your dream, or not, it is probable that you will become involved in some DIY activity after buying your dream house, and thus the customer of a DIY superstore — *Maison de Bricolage* or a *quincaillerie*. There are several chains akin to the familiar B&Q or Texas but carrying a larger range of basic materials and missing out the furniture. Just as in Britain, there are also specialist timber merchants, plumbers and merchants but there are several materials which you may be used to using which do not find their way into the common French inventory and others which will be new to you.

There are many differences in construction methods and styles, some of which can be of considerable significance when you start to alter an existing house. The house, which we fell in love with first, had only an outside lavatory and it was when I started to investigate the feasibility of bringing it indoors and upstairs that one of these came to light. French floors, at least in many older houses, are formed by bridging the space with joists and then by nailing triangular pieces of wood along the bottom of the sides of them so as to form a ledge. This ledge supports a vault made of specially-moulded hollow clay bricks or pots, either single or multiple with a main pot in the middle. The floor above is formed by filling the space above the pots, to level with the top of the joists, with sawdust as sound-deadening and heat insulation and then laying planks across the joists as we are used to. The floor surface may also be made by laying tiles on mortar on top of the pots. Either way it is not feasible to lift up a plank and run cables or pipes or drains in the space between ceiling and floor (which also makes life difficult for mice and reduces draughts). The ceiling surface is made by plastering over the underside of the pots or by lath and plaster in the conventional way.

Another major construction difference lies in the method of attaching the slates to a roof. Whereas we tend to use nails driven through holes in the slates into the supporting battens, the French use wire clips which hook over the batten, come down between the slates of the row beneath and bend up round the bottom of the slate to be fixed. Older roofs will have galvanized steel wire hooks and the galvanizing tends to wear off leaving the clips to rust away. Pay close attention to the clips on the roof of any house you are contemplating buying. Modern buildings use stainless steel which ought to last forever, or plastic coated aluminium. It isn't too difficult a job to replace the clips if the slates themselves are sound but inevitably you will become concerned at the state of the supporting timbers and soon the job will have escalated out of all proportion and become a Concorde-like project into which you are pouring your entire income. Some roofs have their main central areas tiled in the conventional manner for cheapness but use slates for the ridge and hips. Another difference which we came across was the way of forming the ridge to stop the rain getting in. Ridge tiles are uncommon in some areas and a frequently-used method is for both sides of the roof at the ridge to be slated and for the slates on the weather side to be extended out and above those on the lee side of the roof in the shape of an inverted Y. This is not proof against rain ingress in a driving wind and so when our roof was insulated, with foam sprayed under the slates and tiles, it was necessary to form a proper waterproof ridge because any water which got in could not thereafter evaporate easily. In the original it hadn't mattered too much because the roof was so well ventilated that any water which got in would soon evaporate and the pot floor of the loft stopped it penetrating to the interior. Our roofer recommended that the ridge be formed of lead as ridge tiles were not available and I went off in search of sheet lead. Discovery of the day was that the French do not use lead as we do for flashings and gulleys; they prefer to use galvanized sheet steel (or flattened-out old biscuit tins). The search for sheet lead became a challenge which was only solved with the help of an EDF

43

man whom I had met a couple of days previously, whilst he was working in a hole in the road. I was enquiring when power was likely to be restored so that we could boil a kettle. He had been as helpful as an English workman, so accosted, would have been abusive and I met him again in a plumber's merchants as I tried vainly to explain what I wanted and what for. He came to my aid, leading me across town in his barrel-rolling 2CV at breakneck speed from one builder's merchants to another until finally we found some lead and he returned to his job two hours later.

Also on the subject of roofs, the French support their guttering in a different way. You won't often find our usual metal or plastic gutter supported on cantilever brackets fixed to the rafters or a soffit or fascia board — gutters are fixed on the roof itself and form the last, or last but one, row of tiles or slates. They are made of pressed galvanized steel, just like the flashings. This can make them awkward to replace if it is necessary, although the slate clips make it easier to lift a row of slates than if they are nailed.

All dimensions are in the metric system but what is not so expected is the difference in working height of kitchen units. French units seem to be built for midgets and are 5 cm lower than British ones, so remember to allow for this if trying to marry up French and British bits and be prepared for complaints if the units inherited in any house you buy give rise to backache. In practice few French kitchens are fitted to the same extent as in Britain and most are quite rudimentary by comparison.

The French are renowned for their plumbing and this is another area of fundamental difference between them and us. Roof cisterns, full of dead birds or other rubbish, are virtually unknown. The French pressurize their whole plumbing system, both hot and cold, from the mains, and allow any expansion in the hot tank as it is heated to take place by forcing water back into the mains. A safety valve is fitted to the hot tank lest it be heated with all the taps and the main stopcock turned off. The pipework is all executed in what we would regard as microbore copper tube in various sizes according to the likely flow through the system, using capillary and compression fittings which are readily available from the DIY shops. The tube itself comes in coils which can be in the hard or half-hard condition and so difficult to handle. It is easier to manipulate if annealed by heating to redness and allowed to cool or quenched.

Electrical installations are equipped with a *disjoncteur* which is an earth leakage trip combined with an overload trip set to cut out at something above the authorized wattage of your installation. Our house had been professionally rewired and yet the polarity of the wires to the fuse box had been reversed and everything was fused in the neutral, causing me some unexplained shocks until I realized what was the matter. Earth conductors are sheathed in green and yellow within the outer insulation of cables, rather than being left bare as we are used to, and cables are run in convoluted plastic conduit.

Ceiling roses are uncommon and lights frequently hang from a single cable connector but, in general, there are no major differences in practice between the UK and France. Plugs and sockets differ and come in two sizes, with a third smaller size without earth intended solely for lights. Plugs do not contain a fuse. Circuits tend to be on the tree system with individual fuses to each branch as is becoming more common again in England as the IEE changes its mind yet again. Ring circuits are thus an uncommon feature. Earthing may be perfunctory and if in any doubt it will be as well to carry out a thorough check of the resistance to earth of all your socket outlets.

The general dryness of the climate means that there is less emphasis on damp-proof courses than we are used to; downstairs floors are frequently solid with tiled finishes which are cool in summer and can look particularly attractive. If made of unglazed clay tiles such floors can be made to look better — given a perpetual wet look — by swabbing with a mixture of linseed oil and white spirit and allowing to dry. Repeat as necessary. This method avoids the build-up associated with some of the proprietary preparations and allows the floor to breathe.

If dampness does become a problem it is fairly easy to install a dehumidifier; ours runs during the night on off-peak electricity and drains into the main drain so there is no worry about an overflowing container. We leave it on when we are away and it costs very little to run. With a house as near a river as ours the need is real, but in other areas it would not be.

It goes without saying that your windows will probably open inwards, that shutters opening outwards will be fitted with catches to hold them open against the wall. The window furniture will be uniquely French and you may find yourself the possessor of windows which can either open casement style or, if the handles are moved another way, hinge from the top. PVC-U windows don't seem to have caught on except as original fitments in some new houses; probably because the drier climate helps wood to last longer without decay and partly because better quality wood is, or has been, used in the first place. You will soon come to realize that the annual ritual of repainting is one unknown to the French; wood is left to look after itself in the rain and sun.

The forest of matchsticks roof is uncommon, so it is usually possible to use the attic to extend the house, if it is not already part of the accommodation. Once again the drier climate and the greater thickness of the pot floors of lofts mean that there is less preoccupation with the watertightness of the roof — there will frequently be the odd tile or slate missing, often more than one and sometimes a lot. Roof timbers are as prone to woodworm, deathwatch beetle etc. as anywhere else, but once again the structure is so heavily over-engineered that there is plenty for the woodworm to eat without compromising the strength of the roof. They probably finished chomping it many years ago. Sarking felt is uncommon on older roofs and so the foam-bonding system is particularly successful, offering to both fix the slates or tiles and also to add significant insulation against both cold and heat. Our attic is habitable in high summer, now that it is insulated, whereas previously it was like an oven whenever the sun was shining. The French are also keen users of the mansard roof, sometimes with the most beautiful leadwork on dormer windows set into the sloping slate wall-cum roof.

Lavatory cisterns use a different flush system to ours, usually activated by means of a knob on top of the cistern. They can be temperamental but respond to treatment. Basin waste plugs are integral with the outlet and are usually actuated by a knob behind or in between the taps — gone is the plug on a bit of chain, and monobloc taps are common. Showers are easily installed because of the similarity in pressure of the hot and the cold supplies — you won't need to install a booster pump to help the hot supply if the shower is up in the roof. Sanitaryware is priced comparably to that in the UK and comes in a similar variety of colours — either from the DIY shop or from a specialist supplier who will have a greater range to offer but at a higher price.

Because of the high price of heating oil, you will find fewer French houses fitted with pumped water heating systems. The norm is for a wood-burning stove or open grate to be installed in the living room or kitchen (the French are great kitchen-livers) and for the rest of the house to be left to fend for itself or to have electric convectors installed. These can be expensive to run unless they are of the storage type running on off-peak electricity. The wood-burning stoves come in an enormous variety of types and styles; there are extremely elegant enamelled cast iron ones suitable for a medium sized room, often available second hand from a *brocante* if you are lucky. If buying new, a particularly well known and reputable make is Godin. Old ones may need repairs to their mica windows but you can still buy mica from the British Mica Company and replacement is an easy job for any competent DIYer such as you will have become by this time. There are, of course, a lot of larger and more complicated stoves capable of running radiators as well as providing the heat for cooking, just as there are in Britain, if you are planning for super luxury. The real secret lies in securing your supply line — a source of seasoned logs is a must. Finally remember that the French have statutory maximum temperatures allowable in houses of 19°C in living rooms and bathrooms and 18°C in bedrooms. Insulation is accorded a higher priority than in Britain, whether against heat or cold, and many products are on sale which will increase the insulating properties of your building.

For some unfathomable reason, French paint is wickedly expensive and of inferior quality. If ever the French paint manufacturers catch on to how much of the stuff we British are importing into their country to do up our dream houses there will be a paint equivalent of the lamb-burning riots, and gallons of British paint will be tipped into the harbour at Calais. Before they do so, join the club and buy your paint at Texas or B&Q or wherever you fancy and take it over with you.

The French are adept at the use of decorative plaster finishes — and I don't mean Artex. They call it *crépi* and it is a skilled artisan trade and used both outside and in. The problem comes if you need to match an existing area either after alteration or following a repair, because the precise finish may be hard to achieve and will certainly be beyond the average DIYer in his or her first few years. I also had difficulty in getting hold of Thistle or the equivalent finishing plaster from a DIY shop and ended up trying to apply plaster of paris to a wall.

Above all, remember that most rural buildings, and many in towns as well, are PCB — pre-concrete blocks. They will have been built using the local stone and lime mortar and only occasionally will bricks have been used. Stones will only have been dressed in the more prestigious buildings or around the openings such as windows and doors. When you come to knock a small hole in the wall, as we did in order to install a stove in the sitting room, be prepared to come across the most enormous boulder right in the middle of the wall and in the line of your hole. In our case a six-inch diameter opening ended up two feet across and resembled the Channel Tunnel. The danger, if making a larger opening, is of total collapse of an otherwise stable structure if you fail to support it adequately with needles — and getting the needles in, in the first place, can be tricky. This is the time to employ the expert and to check up on his professional insurance beforehand lest your dream house becomes a pile of rubble before your very eyes. Remember, too, to use a comparable mortar mix to the original when making repairs or additions. Modern cements set absolutely rigid and lack the slight flexibility necessary for the survival of old structures built on shallow foundations.

As a general rule you will find the staff of the DIY shops to be helpful in the extreme — none of the vague wave in the direction of the other side of the store and 'I dunno, mate, but they might be over there' in answer to an enquiry for some object not on prominent display. The staff will accompany you until you find what you are looking for and will then be happy to lend you a saw to reduce the timber to a size which will fit the boot of your car, or to saw up sheets of chipboard to convenient and manageable dimensions. All accept credit cards at the till and I have never had any difficulty exchanging anything undamaged or unsoiled, provided I had the receipt.

Finally, remember to take it at a reasonable pace. There will usually be less of a race against the weather, so don't spoil the dream by knocking yourself up — enjoy the sun and keep up your liquid intake.

CHAPTER EIGHT

THE LAW

France is a republic, governed by an elected president (for a seven-year term), a prime minister appointed by the president, and two chambers. As the president and the chambers are not necessarily elected at the same time and, because personality plays a large part in the election of, particularly, the president it can happen that he has to appoint a prime minister of a different political persuasion to himself. This can make for interesting times as it is basically the president who sets the course for the nation, and the government which gives effect to his ideas and wishes. If the two are not of the same opinion the sparks can fly!

The two chambers are the *Assemblée Nationale* which consists of around 577 deputies elected by all enfranchised citizens every five years, and the lesser powered *Sénat* consisting of members elected every nine years by local town councillors.

Beneath the government the country is divided into *départements* — nearly a hundred in all and identified both by name and a number which was their original alphabetical order before later reorganizations added new departments or took away old ones or amalgamated two into one. The numerical alphabetical listing is still pretty accurate, showing the stability enjoyed by this aspect of the organization since its inception. The department number forms the first two digits of the *Cedex* code appearing on letters and roughly equivalent to our postcode, though nowhere near as discriminating in its accuracy.

The country is also divided up into regions, each comprising several *départements*. These can be hard to fathom and confusing as they exist for different purposes — but most are concerned with the promotion of their regional interests in different ways — be it tourism or viticulture or fishing, and they thus represent an amalgamation of areas with a common interest to promote. Some regions are, for this reason, only loosely defined and their boundaries are seldom marked on maps or publications. The town of Château Gontier for example is in the *département* of Mayenne (53) but also lies in the region known as Maine-Anjou. It would also claim to lie in the regions known loosely as Val de Loire and Western Loire so as to benefit from their tourist appeal and the use of the better-known Loire river in their title above its own river, the Mayenne.

While central government determines national policy on major issues, the *départements* enjoy considerable autonomy to raise local taxes and to determine how the money, thus raised, shall be spent. At the head of each *département* is *Le Préfet* and the *Préfecture*, responsible for a wide range of functions which we are used to having performed nationally by a central authority or body. For example, vehicle registration is a departmental responsibility as witnessed by the last two digits of every French car number plate being the *département* identity number.

Beneath the *Préfectures* are the innumerable *Mairies*, some governing hamlets of no more than a few hundred souls while others, usually known by the grander title of *Hôtel de Ville*, are overseeing the governance of a large town or city. The *maire* is an elected official with considerable local powers, often delegated to his officials, but nevertheless it is he who sets the tone and the policy for his area. Being elected a *maire* is thus often the first step in a career in politics and may even lead to election to parliament. It is often the case that the *maire*'s previous career will have been that of notary in his community.

The beauty of this system of regional delegation, for the newcomer, is that no matter what your query concerns, provided you can express yourself well enough in French, it can usually be answered or you can be pointed in the right direction after an enquiry at the local administrative office. If the staff are helpful, the path can prove infinitely smoother than might have been feared at the outset. The office is also where you register births, marriages and deaths (see Chapter 15). Whenever visiting the office it is prudent to take along copies of your residence permit — *Carte de Séjour* — if resident, marriage certificate and any other legal or official document which may have the slightest relevance to the matter in hand. Never part with the originals in any circumstances and most definitely not without obtaining an official receipt — *une quittance* or *un reçu* — for them.

The maintenance of law and order is the responsibility of two basic organizations — the *Gendarmerie Nationale* and the police force, which may be *Nationale* or *Municipale*. The *Gendarmerie* is officially part of the army and is paramilitary in character; it has responsibility for main road policing (where it has power to impose heavy on-the-spot fines of up to FF 5,000 for speeding and even instant disqualification for serious motoring offences), and in country areas where it may be the sole upholder of the law. The *Police Nationale* are not *Gendarmes* (colloquially known as *les flics*) and their officers are properly called *Agents de Police*. They deal with major or serious nationwide criminal investigation and cross all boundaries, leaving local policing of a less serious nature and traffic control to the *Police Municipale* of the town or city.

As a sideline as it were, it is the police who arrange for emergency ambulances and, for this purpose, they can be called on 17. Dialling 18 will connect you with *les Sapeurs Pompiers* who man the rescue and fire services and also spend a lot of their time in other good works such as raising money for charity. In country districts many are part-time and similar to our retained firemen in that they have a full-time job and are called out by sirens or maroons.

The police in towns, and certainly the *Gendarmes*, are slightly distant and awe-inspiring in manner and do not resemble the British bobby in any way at all. In villages it can be another matter, with the local *Agent* or *Gendarme* being a popular member of the community which he polices, and on friendly terms with the citizens of his patch.

If you have the misfortune to be involved in a motoring accident, do not expect the police to attend automatically or take an interest unless someone has been seriously injured or killed. The drivers involved must complete and exchange a form known as a *constat à l'amiable* which you must carry in your car at all times. If using your British insurance you will have been given a European Accident Statement which is the same form under a different name. The insurance companies involved then sort out liability, employing a professional arbitrator-cum-investigator called *un Huissier* if the facts are in dispute. If, however, you suspect that the other party to your accident has been drinking then it is in your own interests to summon the appropriate police — *Gendarmes* or *Agents* according to where you are — and let them breathalyse him. The penalties for drunken driving are comparable to our own with fines of up to FF 30,000 and can be applied arbitrarily by *Gendarmes* on the spot. The alcohol limits are tighter, being 70 mg per litre of blood.

The system of courts has similarities with our own in that there are the equivalent of magistrates' courts for lesser offences and higher courts with juries for the more serious offences. As in the UK, the distinction is drawn between offences against the state and disputes between citizens and, as here, the old maxim coined by John Gay in *The Beggar's Opera*, 'If a lawyer's hand is fee'd, sir, he steals your whole estate,' holds true. Litigation is expensive in France just as it is in the UK and the main beneficiaries are the *avocats* who present and defend the cases. It is to avoid this money-sapping exercise that it is imperative to make sure that there are no outstanding disputes or disagreements concerning boundaries when buying a property.

The penalties for motoring offences include a points system comparable to our own, and points deducted by a French court (and it is only courts which can deduct points) can be taken off a British licence because the French communicate with DVLC. Equally, they can suspend a foreign licence so that its holder can no longer drive in France, so don't think that being a foreigner will let you get away with all sorts of misdemeanours on the roads — it won't. If breathalysed and found to be over the limit you can expect both your licence and your car to be confiscated and you will be left to get to your destination as best you can. If resident and needing your car to follow your profession or trade, an otherwise complete ban on driving can be reduced in severity by the issue of what is known as a *Permis Blanc* which allows you to drive only during working hours and on weekdays. The issue of this sort of licence requires that you have at least one point remaining on your old one. If you have lost points for other offences and have none left then the disqualification will be complete. In the larger cities, you will come across all the measures against illegal car parking that we are used to including clamping and towing-away. It has been claimed that a GB plate is guaranteed to get you towed away if a second over time on a meter on the Côte d'Azur, but in most places the police are fair-minded and helpful.

Those who wish to make a close study of the French political and social scene are recommended to read *France Today* published by Hodder & Stoughton (ISBN 0340557524). This book is regularly updated and is currently in its seventh revised edition.

CHAPTER NINE

YOU AND YOUR MONEY

The need for a French bank account will depend largely on whether or not you are, or intend to become, a full-time resident, though it is perfectly possible to do without a bank account and conduct your finances entirely from Britain. Certainly if you have only a holiday house, visited occasionally and for comparatively short periods, there is little advantage in having a French account. Bills can be paid by Eurocheque, and credit cards allow you to draw cash, as well as pay bills in those places where you are likely to be spending the most — restaurants, DIY shops and supermarkets. Even the village *Huit à Huit* takes Visa.

If, however, you do decide to open an account in France there are several points to consider. First is the choice of bank: the choice basically falls between using a British bank which has a French branch or branches (which will conduct their business to French standards but with a knowledge of your background and circumstances which may prove useful) and an out-and-out French bank. The latter will have more branches throughout the country, which feature may be useful, and it would make sense to choose one with a branch near to your French home.

Nearly all the British high street banks have a branch in France, and Barclays has the most. All, certainly, have a branch in Paris. The French banks fall into two basic classes. There are the equivalent of clearing banks and there are mutual credit organizations, the largest of which is *Crédit Agricole* with branches nationwide and particularly in the smaller towns or villages. There is little difference in the services available to the ordinary domestic customer — both offer cheque accounts and savings accounts and can provide mortgage assistance if needed. There are also banks which operate only as savings banks — *Caisse d'Epargne* being a typical example.

Your first account will perforce be a non-resident account and this will be the case for the first two years, after which it will become an ordinary account and some rather irksome restrictions will be removed. These include a ban on overdrafts. In France it is a serious offence to write a cheque if there are insufficient funds in the account to meet it. If you bounce a cheque you are given 30 days in which to put the account back into credit (and don't expect to be given an overdraft in order to do it), failing which your account will be frozen for a year and you will be banned from writing cheques for up to ten years and fined 12% of the amount of the bouncing cheque. Your details are passed to the *Banque de France* in case you try to open an account with another bank, and if you do try then the police are notified. Cheques cannot be post-dated and neither can they be stopped; they automatically expire after one year and eight days.

Credit cards, as we commonly call them, are not widely used; the French equivalent is a charge card akin to Switch, of which by far the most common is *Carte Bleue*. British Visa cards are almost universally accepted as charge cards, despite the fact that in strict terms they are credit cards as far as we are concerned. The point is that the retailer is guaranteed his funds, and that is all he is concerned about. The larger stores are on line to the issuing authority and so it is not possible to exceed the credit limit. For a transaction fee and, with a PIN, the same cards also enable you to draw cash from dispensers — *guichets* — in most banks and the larger post offices. These too are on-line and will not allow you to draw more than the issuing authorities' rules permit, so it is worthwhile to check up on the small print of your card. The big advantage of using a British credit card is the normally excellent rate of exchange. If your principal source of income is in sterling this can be of considerable importance.

The main disadvantage in using a card is the risk of loss; if your card falls into unscrupulous hands it is possible for it to be used to obtain goods on your account and the fraud is unlikely to be detected because the French are remarkably slack over comparing signatures on the card and the voucher. A good insurance against misuse can be worth its weight in gold.

Eurocheques are comparatively expensive, especially if used for small amounts, but they are useful for paying French bills from Britain and of course can be used for paying bills in France or getting cash out of a bank.

If you decide to open an account in France, you will need to be able to provide proof of your identity — a passport will usually suffice, and it may help to have your birth certificate available as well, together with the residence permit, if you have one. It may even help to have the deeds of your house, if you have already bought it. Once your account is opened, don't expect things to be done as quickly as we are used to. Cheques can take several days to clear and be credited to an account. Funds can be transferred from Britain, if that is your income source, by simple instruction to your British bank who will need to know your account number and name and the identity code of the recipient bank.

Your French account should entitle you to a *Carte Bleue* or equivalent, which is preferred to personal cheques by many stores, but remember the absolute necessity to stay in credit, so keep careful account of your use of the card.

Exchange controls between Britain and France are now a thing of the past but the rate can still vary in response to the pressures of the market and if transferring a large amount a good crystal ball can save a worthwhile sum.

Income tax exists in France just as in Britain and is payable on all income arising in the country, regardless of residential status. In theory you are liable to pay tax on any rent earned by letting your house to visitors, and it is here that the double taxation agreements between Britain and France come to your help to prevent both countries trying to levy tax on the same income. In France you are obliged to register with the *Centre des Impots de Non-Residents* and it may become necessary for them to resolve your tax liability with your British office if, for example, both authorities are trying to claim tax on rent or other income arising in France while you are still considered a British resident.

The French will consider you to be a resident for tax purposes if any of the following criteria are met — there is no choice in the matter:

(a) You have a home in France in which you spend more than 183 days per year, or where you spend more time than you spend in any other home no matter where it may be.

(b) You earn money from employment (including self-employment) in France unless the occupation in France is auxiliary to a main employment elsewhere.

(c) Your income arises from French sources, e.g. French stocks and shares.

If you are earning in France there will be little doubt concerning your liability to pay tax in that country and the system will be found to have both similarities and differences to the British system. There is an allowance of tax-free income above which tax is levied at ever-increasing rates as income rises. Allowances exist for married couples and for children and it is advisable to take professional advice if your tax affairs are complicated.

As the British owner of a French property you will be exempt from paying French tax on any rents earned from it by virtue of the double tax treaty which exists between the two countries: but remember that this assumes that you are declaring the income to the British tax authorities.

If you earn an income in France you should be aware of the fact that tax is levied on the basis of the previous year's income, with adjustments being made when actual income for a particular year becomes known. The tax return has to be rendered by 28 February each year and the assessed tax is payable in three instalments. The first two are based entirely on the previous year's tax bill and are each equal to one-third of it: they are payable on 15 February and 15 May, with the third and final instalment claimed in September.

A second system exists whereby the tax is paid by direct debit from a bank account with a tenth of the previous year's total tax being taken on the 8th of the month from January to October. The final balancing payments are taken in November and December. This method has the advantage of spreading payment over the year more evenly and it removes the worry of remembering to send off the payments, but it prevents you from earning interest on the money for quite as long.

Whatever system you use, it is vital to be able to pay the tax, due on income earned in the past, when it is demanded, even if you have since become unemployed and are no longer earning.

If you are resident in France after your retirement, it should be remembered that any pension income from British sources, including state old-age pension, will be taxed in France rather than in Britain unless it is from the British government in respect of government service, e.g. a pension from HM Armed Forces. Pensions paid for government service are always taxed at source in Britain.

French inheritance tax will be payable on your estate when you die and if you have become a French resident your whole worldwide estate will be liable for it — or rather the beneficiaries under your will become liable for the tax on their portions. If you are merely a French property owner then the tax will only be levied on your possessions in France. There is no exemption for bequests to your spouse but the biggest difference in the system lies in the fact that the tax is levied on the beneficiaries under the deceased's will and the rates charged vary according to the closeness of their relationship as well as the amount received. This system was intended to preserve the fortunes of families by offering a disincentive to will estates outside the family. A surviving spouse for example has the first FF 330,000 worth of bequest tax free and then pays tax on a sliding scale with a top rate of 40%, while other close relatives will get a tax-free allowance of FF 300,000 and then a similar sliding scale. More distant relatives, and this category includes brothers and sisters, get a tax-free allowance of only FF 10,000 and a more punitive sliding scale.

Just as in Britain, personal tax is a complicated business with generalization impossible and even potentially misleading. It is vital to take advice from a suitably qualified person who is familiar with the regimes in both countries and who fully understands your position and your intentions. In particular it is imperative that there be no mistake or confusion over the question of your domicile, i.e. where you are regarded as resident. This has enormous implications for both your income tax liability and your estate on death, and it is vital that there shall be no possibility of argument over it and that it is as you wished and intended when organizing your affairs.

What is certain is that moving to France is no way to escape or evade paying tax of any kind, and that the liability in either country is of comparable size.

Still on the subject of tax, the French equivalent of VAT is called *TVA*. It is charged at three rates of 5.5%, 18.6% and a luxury rate of 28%. Interestingly the luxuries are deemed to include cars, jewellery and pornography, while food and hotel bills attract *TVA* at the lowest rate. The different rates of *TVA* account for many of the price differentials between Britain and France and may be expected to diminish as the Brussels machine exerts more and more of its harmonizing influence over Europe.

The post office and postal system in France is generally dependable, if a little slower than we are used to. The equivalent of postcodes is a system called the *Cedex*. This is a five-digit code, the first two being the *département* number and the remaining three denoting an area or town within it. It is nowhere near as discriminating as postcodes (which are accurate to within about six houses in some places), but its omission will delay a letter considerably. What is worth remembering, however, is the French propensity for claiming that any unwelcome communication never arrived. If it is important to be able to prove that a letter was delivered it is essential that you register it at the post office when sending it off. If calling to collect an undelivered letter or packet (maybe you were out or the postman didn't fancy the climb to your door on the twelfth floor to deliver in person) you will need to be able to prove your identity by means of your passport or residence permit. Postage rates are broadly comparable to those in Britain, but never use the French second class tariff.

Finally a word about Capital Gains Tax. It exists in France just as in Britain and is worked on a roughly similar set of principles in calculating the chargeable gain — provable expenses in renovation can be deducted and so can a proportion of the purchase price for expenses and there are allowances for family but thereafter the tax is payable on the disposal of second homes. The good news is that although the tax is levied at a basic rate of 33.3% you are allowed to reduce the gain by 5% for each year of ownership after three, so the moral is to choose wisely and stay in your dream home for 23 years. Those who are restoring houses for profit are advised to take advice — it will probably be to their advantage to live in the property, currently being restored, as their main residence. But only an expert can advise you. Remember that, by definition, you will be regarded as a French resident for tax purposes, if working in the country.

CHAPTER TEN

MAKING A LIVING

Except for the fortunate few whose independent means allow them to refrain from work, or the retired, living on an adequate pension, it will be necessary to find some way of earning or supplementing your income in France. Working or entering commerce in any shape or form is also a particularly good way of getting to meet people and make friends.

The typical dream of the good life in France includes taking in a few B&B guests to help supplement the income from a pension or investments, and this can often work out very well, but there are a few points to be aware of if your enterprise gets any larger than the occasional guest. First, the income must be declared for tax either in France or the UK. If you live in France for more than six months a year then you are regarded as resident for tax purposes and must declare the income in that country to the French tax authorities.

If non-resident, you have the choice, and it will probably be easier, to add it in with your declaration at home. Whether to declare the income in the UK, or in France, will be influenced by the different tax treatments of the two countries. If declared in the UK you are unlikely to receive any more by way of a tax allowance than the possibility — and it depends on your Inspector — of allowing the interest on a loan to buy the property to be offset for tax. If declared in France you will have to pay *TVA* on the rents received at 5.5% but, thereafter, you will be able to claim for the loan interest (if in francs and taken out in France), depreciation of the property itself at 4% and management fees charged by an agent and for advertising as well as for maintenance, repairs and cleaning and even for visits to inspect the property. When doing your sums, beforehand, it can be fatal to be too optimistic and to overestimate the length of the season or your room-occupancy rate. If you are aiming to appeal to families, they will only be capable of coming during the school holidays and few will come at Easter unless you have something special to attract them like the mating season of the lesser vermilion-backed tortoise unique to your garden. In high summer most visitors will expect a swimming pool and the running costs of this can be high, especially if you have to employ someone to give it its essential daily clean. Remember, too, the absolute necessity for adequate insurance and allow for the premium in your calculations. If taking out this insurance in France be sure to retain the services of a reputable broker and be absolutely certain that you understand all the small print. Be prepared, also, to have to employ someone to do some of the chores. It is all too easy for the dream to turn sour if you find yourself tied to the house and its environs because of the demands of the pool or of any other facilities you have installed to attract your guests. Can you bear to be working while your guests are enjoying themselves in the paradise you had found for yourself?

Another major expense, to attract guests, will be advertising, and here you enter a veritable minefield. Where to advertise and when to do it for maximum effect; how to measure its effectiveness and how much to budget for in any one year are all unanswerable questions. Many owners abroad take what may be seen as the easy route and employ an agent who will put their property in a portfolio which they market professionally — and, of course, take a share of your profits for their pains. If you are going to be on hand to oversee the lettings, life will, at least, be that little bit easier than if you are letting, while yourself, staying in Britain, though it will be that much harder to communicate with your British contacts unless you install a fax machine. Many of the ferry companies now run French letting packages and you may find it convenient to enlist their aid, but you will need someone reliable on the spot to see guests in and out and to see to the laundry and any minor defects. As an absentee landlord — in the final analysis — unless you need to make a lot of money, it may be best to restrict your letting to a small circle of clients who know that they are renting an unsupervised holiday house and who take their own bed linen. Friends of mine have done this successfully for a couple of years, advertising in a select magazine circulated only within their former profession, so they can hope at least that their guests will be house trained.

If you are really doing it as a business, then, don't underestimate the wear and tear on the furnishings and fabric; mattresses for example will need to be replaced after a few years and any fittings or equipment used by guests need to be robust and functional. Choose china and cutlery which are easily replaceable at reasonable cost and preferably available locally. Easy-iron bed linen and tolerant carpets are absolute musts. If you aim for an international clientele rather than an exclusively British one, remember too, that the Continentals tend to keep their children up far later than we do, so be prepared for them to be running around making a noise when you might be wishing them abed. It goes without saying that an international clientele will require a matching fluency in languages on your part, at least in French. The upside to establishing a holiday letting business is the existence of a wide range of possible grants for converting old buildings into *gîtes*. Ask at your local *mairie* first and they will be able to point you in the right direction if they do not have any funds so earmarked. There are several potential sources ranging up to EEC funds in some areas.

The lowering of barriers within the EEC means that in theory, at least, it is now possible to seek employment in France without needing a work permit. You will need a residence permit if staying in the country for more than six months and this entitles you to seek work. France is several years behind Britain in coming out of recession and jobs are not plentiful. However, it will be easier to find one if you target an occupation for which you are uniquely qualified and for which there will be few French applicants; so don't try to become a Breton fisherman. One such is the teaching of English in schools or privately at home, but you will need a recognized TEFL qualification just as you will need the appropriate qualification for any professional post for which you apply. If applying for jobs in the normal way you will of course need a CV in French, made out to conform to the expected layout and conventions, and the covering letter will again need to be in French and to conform to the very particular conventions of business correspondence. If unfamiliar with these, consult a French-speaker or the *Collins-Robert* dictionary. It contains a most useful guide to the nuances of business letters and forms of address, besides being an extremely comprehensive dictionary complete with many idiomatic and vernacular translations in both directions which may help keep you out of unwitting trouble.

If entering paid employment, you will discover that there is virtually no dictinction made between what we would regard as salaried and wage-paid jobs. Almost all employees are paid monthly, less deductions for social security — *sécurité sociale*. The process of finding a job is little different to that in the UK but is perhaps a trifle more formal, with interviews being involved in filling more lowly positions than would be considered normal here. Interviews are taken particularly seriously, with personal appearance counting for a lot. The contract of employment, however, will assume more than usual importance as it will be the proof of your having obtained employment which will be demanded by the authorities when you apply for a residence permit, if you are under retirement age. It should, of course, specify all the expected facts concerning your employment and is a legal requirement. In particular, it should specify the terms of cancellation since your redundancy payment — if things come to that — will depend on them.

If you land a job, remember that there is no system of PAYE in France. You will be required to account for your earnings to the tax authorities and be able to pay them the tax due within a short time of their demand for payment. So don't spend every franc as soon as you earn it.

Just as there are a few jobs for which an English person in France is uniquely qualified, so there are some which only the exceptional or the foolhardy will attempt. There are not many English restaurants in France; black pudding, Cumberland sausage, Cornish pasties, Yorkshire pudding and mushy peas have not caught on and it will be a brave person who tries to introduce them to the French. You might set up a successful pie shop in a centre visited by lots of British tourists, but is that really your dream? By the same token, there aren't many British ski instructors; the French have got that pretty well sewn-up among themselves, as they have the windsurfing instruction on the Côte d'Azur. But you might be successful working at a Club Med village visited by many British, and there can be few more congenial ways of improving your command of the language because all Club Med villages, in France, are run in French.

If starting up any business, remember the need for adequate working capital and be prepared for various tax authorities to make over-optimistic estimates of your probable tax liability, particularly *TVA*, and to ask for considerable sums on account. If setting yourself up in any artisan trade — *métier* — you will need to be able to show that you have received a full trade training or completed an indentured apprenticeship before you will be allowed to trade. Having done a TOPS course or some other short training will not usually be enough — the French are still keen on full, trade training for their artisans and protect those who are qualified from unqualified cowboy competition. It will also be necessary to be acceptably qualified in order to be able to join a friendly society — *mutuelle* — connected with your trade and thus to benefit from their additional health insurance if you fall sick.

There are various levels of business just as there are in Britain. Starting with the sole trader — *entreprise individuelle* — one progresses to the limited liability company whose equivalent is the *Société à Responsabilité Limitée (SARL)*. This requires anything between two and fifty directors and a minimum capital of FF 50,000. If you outgrow your *SARL* you must become a *Société Anonyme*, requiring a capital of not less than FF 250,000 and a properly constituted board of directors. By this time you will be able to retain the services of an *avocat* to advise you on the legal niceties of your operation.

Partnerships are governed by very complex rules and precedents and expert advice is required before entering into one. Whatever form your operation takes, it is necessary to register with the local Chamber of Commerce — *Syndicat d'Initiative* — and the Commercial Register. The *mairie* will point you in their direction if you get stuck.

If you employ any staff, it is imperative that you become aware of French employment legislation. A most useful source of information on this, and on all aspects of setting-up in business in France, is the government organization called *DATAR — Délégation à l'Aménagement du Territoire et à l'Action Régionale* — whose address in Britain is given on page 105. The existence of this organization and its possession of a London office shows the keenness of the French on encouraging the establishment of small businesses, and not just by the French.

Buying an existing business is perfectly feasible and all the precautions appropriate to such a purchase in Britain apply equally in France. The actual formalities are not very different to those involved in buying a property but the legal fees will be higher and may amount to as much as 20% of the price. It is possible to buy an existing business in rented premises and take over the lease on them, taking appropriate advice from a notary on the way!

Whatever business you may end up running or owning, it is important to engage the services of an accountant who is familiar with the bureaucratic demands made on such enterprises. It will be worth everything charged, as you will be steered through the maze of returns and forms which will descend on you from officialdom. VAT officers are no less efficient in France than in Britain.

The payments made for social security also entitle you to unemployment benefit — *ASSEDIC* or *Allocation d'assurance chômage* — but only if they have been made for at least three months or 520 working hours in the last 12 months. The benefit is usually paid at 40% of previous earnings while sick pay is 50%. If the claimant is unemployed and drawing unemployment benefit in Britain it is theoretically possible to transfer the entitlement to France and draw benefit there at British rates for up to three months while seeking work. The process starts with a visit to your local benefits agency office in Britain who in turn contact their overseas branch from whom you should receive a form E303 which you take to France. In France, take the form to Social Security or even your local town hall and hope they are in a co-operative mood. If not, get set for a long struggle. At the end of the three months the entitlement runs out and without a residence permit, or the ability to support yourself for another three months as a tourist, you will have to come home.

It is probably true to say that the three months' contributions rule which effectively prevents young persons from leaving home without means of supporting themselves has contributed as much as anything to the preservation of the family in France. Children tend to live at home for the first few years of their adult life and only leave if their work actually takes them away, or they get married.

Becoming a wine-grower — *vigneron* — has a certain appeal and can sound very attractive when telling your friends, in the gin-and-Jaguar belt, of your plans to live in France, but this too can be an overrated activity and is fraught with hazards for the unknowledgeable or the naive. Remember that grape-growing, like every other farming activity, is dependent on the weather. A hailstorm at the wrong time can destroy, in ten minutes, a whole year's work and expense and effort by way of pruning, repairing the wirework, spraying against this and that, thinning, cultivating between the rows etc. The long-established wine-growers have built up reserves to tide them over such occasional adversity, but if it hits you in your first or second year will you be able to cope?

Having got a crop of grapes they have to be of a certain minimum sugar content before the co-operative will buy them for wine making or before you can make wine yourself. Otherwise they go to make industrial alcohol etc., at a greatly reduced price. Sugar content can change almost overnight, and it is not something that can be left to itself; vines need almost as much attention as a baby if they are to give a worthwhile return. If making your own wine, within an *appellation contrôlée*, you will need to satisfy the overseers of the *appellation* continually that your product is up to scratch and that your premises meet the latest regulations. On top of this there is always the question of the vintage and whether it is a good year or not for wine in general. In other words, are you going to be able to sell it at a profit after meeting all the costs of production? In those costs of production must be included the cost of all the extensive machinery which you will have acquired. Sprayers, pruners, wire stretchers, tractors, trailers, presses, vats, bottling and labelling plant all cost a lot of money, although used for only a few weeks each year. It is possible to hire some of the machines, but that makes you dependent on the hirer and, at peak times, when you may be desperate to spray against mildew, the hirer may not be able to oblige. Self-sufficiency has a lot to recommend it but it comes at a price. Incidentally, you are also liable for the tax on your wine and have to account for the little foil seals which are folded or crimped around the neck of each bottle.

When it all comes together though, there can be few pleasures to beat a juicy steak barbecued over a fire of old vine roots. If washed down with your own wine whilst you sit in the dappled shade of an old olive tree and the balmy warmth of an evening in the Dordogne or Burgundy, the dream will have come true.

CHAPTER ELEVEN

VIVE LA DIFFÉRENCE

There are many differences in culture and behaviour between us Anglo-Saxons and the French. Some are obvious and others are more subtle but it is worth spending a little time studying them so as to avoid the possibility of giving unwitting offence.

We have all seen the customary cheek-kissing exercise — which virtually all French people indulge in on meeting — but do you know which cheek to kiss first or how many pecks to give? If ever there was a typical example of a custom where it is possible to make errors through ignorance of the form, this is it because the conventions of which cheek to kiss first, and how many pecks to give, vary from region to region and from time to time.

First, one should be sure that one's acquaintance with the lady in question is sufficiently close that offence will not be given by the mere attempt. Once over that hurdle, study the form and the number of pecks given by others or, if in doubt, take your cue from the lady herself. If she continues to offer her cheek — give her another peck, swopping from side to side with each one. Men, greeting one another simply shake hands, but are much more ready to do it than we are used to. The offered handshake can be expected from virtually anyone met for the first time every day. I regularly shake hands with our village dustman, who also doubles up as roadsweeper, when he calls to empty the bin or I pass him in the street on my way back from the baker with the fresh *croissants* for breakfast.

Attending to calls of nature in public is another activity of fundamental difference that the usually reserved British find a little unusual. Whereas most of us will scale a barbed wire fence, brave a field of bulls and hide behind the most distant big tree that we can find, before relieving ourselves, our French counterpart will quite, unashamedly, stand right beside the road with traffic roaring past. The ladies tend to be a bit more discreet, but not greatly so. The *Clochemerle* type of urinal, or *pissotière* to give it its French name, is found almost everywhere, catering for the men, and it makes few concessions to modesty or privacy but is eminently practical. However if freshly sanitized and disinfected premises are a necessity for you, then a certain amount of difficulty can be foreseen unless you are fortunate enough to find one of the new space-age contraptions, which now adorn some of the larger railway stations and public spaces. For FF 5, these give you the ultimate in modern facilities — but don't linger too long, lest you get caught up in the cleansing cycle which comes between each usage!

Entertaining in the home is an activity where again our two cultures have a divergence. The Frenchman seldom invites any but his closest and oldest friends to eat at home indoors with him. He will prefer to spend a considerable amount of money entertaining friends in a restaurant or café, often for lunch on Sunday. This is by no means a hard-and-fast rule, but nevertheless it is usually a particular sign of friendship to be invited to dine in a French house, though the reluctance to entertain at home diminishes as one rises up the social and wealth ladders. Eating outdoors is another matter and, of course, the generally better weather and climate make this a more dependable activity — there is a reasonable chance that an event can be planned in advance, with some confidence that it won't be rained off. Eating out of doors can be a special pleasure in itself and even the humblest picnic is usually turned into a gourmet event with the wine flowing and the conversation suddenly seeming to be a lot easier as traditional English reserve is overcome with the help of a little *vin du pays*. Some villages have a communal meal outdoors to mark the occasion of Bastille Day — *le quatorze juillet* — and this is a treat not to be missed. The tables will groan under the weight of delicious local specialities, the wine will flow and bonhomie will be all-pervasive. This is *la vie Française* at its best.

The French attitude to their children also marks them as

different to the British: it is common to see toddlers still up and about at 10 p.m. and they, and infants in arms, are frequently taken into restaurants while their parents dine at a late hour, when ours would long have been abed. I have seen a playpen, taken through a restaurant for the use of a diner's small child, occupying a hall at the back of the establishment, and not a hair seemed to be turned by the other diners. This precocity is not normally matched by any unpleasantness of manner as they grow older: French children seem to value their family ties and to respect their elders more than we now expect. The tragedy is, that for the less well educated, the prospects of getting a stable and enduring job are becoming ever more remote and, while there are as yet few signs of active discontent, it can only be a matter of time.

The family remains a strong unit, despite the wide dispersion of its members in many instances. Members will travel long distances to be together for reunions on Saints days and to celebrate birthdays and anniversaries — usually with a meal.

It was with the preservation of families and their wealth that another particular feature of French life was established, namely the *Code Napoléon* which specifies the way in which property is to be handed down from one generation to another, and the portions of a deceased's estate to which successors are entitled. The significance of this, for the incomer, is that whatever property you own in France it will be handled according to the *Code Napoléon* when you die. If no will has been made, then the estate will be divided up between the entitled beneficiaries immediately and the first problem which may be encountered is that a surviving spouse has no automatic right to all the deceased partner's estate. If the survivor is a wife, the estate will be divided between her and her children and relatives according to a set formula which will give her, probably, only one quarter of the estate. This can be overcome only by making a French will, drawn up so as to leave the deceased's estate to the surviving spouse in trust for his or her lifetime and then, on the death of the second partner, according to the *Code Napoléon* to the children or other relatives. If non-resident, the will should be drawn up specifically to cover only the legator's French property and if, as is usual, the property is owned by a man and wife as *copropriétaires*, it is perfectly feasible to arrange a *usufruit* or a *donation entre époux* by which the survivor inherits the whole estate for his or her lifetime. Matters may have been made easier if you have purchased the property *en tontine* and it is wise to seek the advice of your notary at the time of purchase rather than putting it off to some later and, probably forgotten, date. Nobody likes the discipline of facing up to the inevitability of their death, but failure to do so in France can have very unusual and, to our way of thinking, sometimes unwelcome effects.

The easiest and most reliable way to draw up a will is to use your notary who will charge about FF 1,000 for his services. Make sure that he knows of the existence of your British will and equally let your British executors know of the existence of your French will.

In England the executors of a will take temporary charge of the estate and then distribute it, in accordance with the terms of the will, having authority to do what they need by way of disposing of assets given to them by the will. In France this is not so — the beneficiaries immediately assume the right to their portion even if it is a fraction of a house or land, and it is the inability to agree to dispose of a house held by several beneficiaries which is one of the reasons why one sees so many seemingly abandoned properties around the countryside. There is no equivalent to our probate system and it is not essential to appoint executors, though it can be useful if your assets are to pass to people who are not themselves French or resident in France.

It is possible to draw up a will yourself without using a notary. This is called a *testament olographe* and it must be written and dated in your own handwriting. It must not be witnessed by anyone at all and must all be in your handwriting. With the risk of making some fatal flaw in its drafting, this can be a difficult business and the notarial method is probably money well spent. Note that marriage does not automatically invalidate any previous will as it does in the UK, so it may be necessary to be specific about revoking any previous wills when making a first French one. Leave the will with your notary, or with your British solicitor if you are not a full-time resident.

If you have become a resident, or have assumed residence for tax purposes, then all your worldwide possessions will become subject to your French will and it is even more important that you make one if your successors are to be spared untold difficulty and even hardship after your death. This is another reason for making quite sure that there is no possible ambiguity as to your residence, because if you don't consider yourself to be resident but the taxman does, then the arguments can go on for years with your nearest and dearest left waiting for their inheritance or even being assessed for tax on a house in Britain, which you expected to be dealt with under British law. Remember that in France, it is the individual beneficiaries who pay inheritance tax at varying rates on their inheritance. Basically, the further removed they are from you in relational terms the more they pay.

When the inevitable happens and it is time for your will to be put into effect, it has merely to be given to a notary and he will see to its filing with the appropriate authorities, alteration of the deeds as necessary to record the change of ownership of a house and/or land and the collection of inheritance tax will follow as night follows day. For the other formalities following a death, see Chapter 15.

It is a popular misconception that the English are the only nation to love dogs. There are, in fact, more pampered pooches in France than in England but the British anti-rabies regulations make it impossible to take pets from here to France and bring them back again without quarantine. This law may be changed in the very near future, so it will be as well to keep up to date with the current regulations as it may become possible for the Francophile pussy cat to cross the Channel with ease. Rabies is seldom, if ever, encountered in France but it is, nevertheless, unwise to approach any stray or distressed dog.

Inoculations are mandatory against rabies, hardpad and distemper for dogs, and against typhus and feline gastroenteritis for cats, and if your pet has not had these before departure, so that they are still in date, they must be administered immediately on arrival. It will help your acceptance, if the dose or batch number of the rabies vaccine is tattooed on the inside of the animal's ear, a required practice in

France. When taking your pet to France, it is necessary to have with you a certificate obtained from a vet registered with the MAFF no more than five days prior to your departure, certifying your pet as clear of rabies. Alternatively take a certificate from the MAFF itself certifying that Britain has been free of rabies for the three previous years and that your animal has lived in Britain since its birth or for the last six months. The French also limit you to the importation of three pets, as a maximum, at a time.

French parks are subject to the same regulations as our own and it is obligatory to keep dogs on a leash in them. In the country, take the same precautions as you would at home to prevent your pet worrying stock or neighbours — farmers will be more inclined to shoot and ask questions afterwards than we are used to if they come across a dog chasing their sheep or wild deer. Well-behaved animals can be taken into restaurants and will be made a fuss of.

The French have a reputation for being chic. In Paris this is undoubtedly well deserved but, out in the country, it is perhaps less so. Nevertheless the average Frenchwoman is usually better dressed than has become the norm in Britain of late, and this despite the far greater expense of clothes in France. By and large the French wardrobe will contain fewer clothes but of better quality. There is no equivalent of M&S, although they have themselves opened a number of stores in France, but the major supermarket chains offer a wide variety of everyday clothes. Most towns will have a couturier for the ladies, and some now boast shops selling second-hand designer clothes. Most open-air markets will have an abundance of clothes for both sexes on sale from a van with lift-up sides and a sliding roof which expands, on arrival, to as much as six times its basic floor area.

CHAPTER TWELVE

LEISURE AND PLEASURE

The stereotype image of the Frenchman's leisure is, naturally enough, centred on wine drinking and the playing of *pétanque* (a form of bowls), and it isn't all that far from the truth. *Pétanque* or *boules*, as it is commonly known, is the universal pastime of all ages and classes and is played with passion by its devotees. Most villages, particularly in the south, have an area set aside for the game but it can be, and frequently is, played almost anywhere and on any surface. Tournaments such as those immortalized in Marcel Pagnol's novels are organized in summer, frequently as part of a larger fête or fair.

Perhaps the second most popular sporting activity is cycling, with the *Tour de France* representing its pinnacle. Lesser races and trials are organized all over the country and are followed with keenness and devotion. The convoy, which precedes any group of racers on the road, has to be seen to be believed, and the sport is heavily commercialized.

On a quieter and more sedate level are the multitude of fishermen who line the bank of virtually any stretch of water in any weather with an optimism which belies description. Fishing is said to be the pastime with the largest following of all and it attracts devotees of all ages and both sexes. It is certainly big business for the shops selling the inevitable impedimenta of the sport. Anyone can try their hand and the only licence necessary can be purchased from the *tabac* for a few francs.

Association football has a devoted following, mainly in bars and around the television though most villages and towns have a pitch and a club, and rugby football similarly has a group of fans. Neither game has the depth of following experienced in Britain. Golf, however, is a growth sport and courses are being built in more and more places. Some are pretty expensive, depending on the extent of local demand for membership. The local tourist office — *Office du Tourisme* — will be able to tell you of any courses in your region if Yellow Pages can't help.

The tourist office is, in fact, the source of information on the enormous variety of cultural events which take place almost everywhere, ranging from the local village *fête* in aid of the church roof fund to fabulous displays of *Son et Lumière* in the grand houses and *châteaux*. Concerts in the open air, historical pageants, art exhibitions, craft shows, antiques fairs, theatre performances and cinemas all flourish and can be tremendous fun. Many of these pageants are linked to the cultural heritage of which most of the French are intensely proud.

The key to the enjoyment of any of these events is directly related to your command of the language: but don't let any lack of skill in this direction deter you from attending as many events and functions as possible. You may not understand all the nuances of the dialogue, or all the jokes, but the experience will be fun and your French is bound to improve. If your French is fairly good, and you are so inclined, there is often a local amateur dramatic group to join and what better way to get to know your neighbours and to make friends among them. You don't, necessarily, have to have acting ambitions — there is lots to do backstage, just as in any theatre club. Professional theatre does not seem to flourish outside the very large towns to any significant extent.

For lovers of the great outdoors, many tourist centres have walking and cycling circuits of varying degrees of length or difficulty or challenge, laid out and documented while, if you are a lover of the water, the country is riddled with rivers, many of them navigable by power craft and, even more, by canoe or kayak. There is also a network of working canals, mainly in the east. Many of the lesser rivers, which may not be navigable are, nevertheless, the focus of inland leisure areas with canoes for hire, swimming facilities and always a well laid-out picnic area. Larger lakes are frequently made into centres for sailing in dinghies or on sailboards, which may be hired, as well as for swimming and, of course, fishing.

Many smaller lakes are also stocked for fishing alone and it is common to see the *passionnés de la pêche* huddled under their umbrellas in the rain with eyes fixed on the float. The dedicated dry-fly angler might look down his nose at the lures in common use and the amount of ground bait used to tempt the quarry. The species of fish, too, are unfamiliar to those accustomed to dangling their hook in a British canal or river, but several make good eating.

Caravanning and camping are popular and the country is well served by a variety of camp sites varying from the small and basic to the luxurious. They will be found on the banks of the larger rivers and lakes, in particular. All contain washing facilities and lavatories and the larger, and better equipped, will have power points and even water connections at each pitch. Pitches will be separated from one another by hedges and the layout is usually spacious and pleasant. The charges are modest in the extreme — a few francs in some cases. Some town and city dwellers will move their entire household out to a camp site for the whole summer and the breadwinner will commute to work on a daily or weekly basis for the duration of the school holidays and join his or her family full time for the annual holiday. In any case, the French holiday calendar means that the vast majority of workers take a long break of three or four weeks in the summer, keeping only a week or so for Christmas or Easter. All workers are entitled to five weeks' holiday each year.

Serious boating is possible on the navigable rivers, either in your own boat trailed across — sailed across if large enough — or hired from one of the several firms offering *bateaux sans permis* — meaning no licence is required. If taking your own boat to France the law requires that VAT be paid on it if you become a full-time resident, or if it is to remain in the country and be used for more than a total of six months in a year, regardless of your residential status, or if it is to be hired out, with the arrangements for the hire or charter being made in France, or if it is to be hired to someone French, no matter where the arrangements are made. On the rivers there are no charges to use the waterway, to go through the locks (which are all operated for you by lock keepers) or to moor for the night. There is very little traffic, by the standards of any British river, and the scenery is mostly delightful. In the south the scene is rather different, with marina berths being at a premium and expensive. The rules for VAT apply, as above, and are more likely to be rigorously enforced by the local Customs. Most of the larger and navigable rivers have a speed limit of 10 kph but this is relaxed in stretches set aside for water-skiing which is popular throughout the country.

The French have instituted a system of licensing for skippers of boats but, at the time of writing, it is not applied to skippers of foreign registered boats. There is thus some benefit to be gained by flying the 'Red Duster' and having your craft officially registered in the UK — probably on the Small Ships Register which is run for the DOT by DVLC at Swansea. For once, if you have become a French resident, the Red Ensign becomes a flag of convenience!

Tennis, too, is a popular sport and courts for hire will be found in the unlikeliest places. Most villages, nowadays, have a *salle de sports* or *salle polyvalente* which is the centre of sporting activity and home to the local football team and other games such as badminton or volley-ball. It is the equivalent of the better of our village halls and may also be used for social events.

For lovers of racing and horses, in addition to the well-known international events, such as the *Prix de l'Arc de Triomphe*, there are many little racecourses dotted around the country. Not only flat racing and steeplechasing are practised but also trotting, which is especially popular in the Orne area. The courses are mostly small affairs, holding two or three meetings a year but in beautiful settings. I recall, particularly, the course at Le Lion d'Angers in Maine-et-Loire which is right next door to the national stud on the Ile de Briand. Set on the fringe of the town, the course runs beside the river and is a delightful spot in which to spend a day with a picnic on the grass, a bottle or two of wine in the cold box and a couple of hot tips in your pocket.

Much of the countryside is ideal for riding and most rural properties, if not blessed with stables, will have some grazing and space to put up a loose box or two.

La chasse — hunting — is popular throughout the country

and involves the hunting of deer or, in some areas, wild boar, as well as game birds and waterfowl. If you come across signs stating *chasse gardée* or *chasse privée* and they look reasonably new be careful how you proceed because the French are far more touchy about trespass than we are in Britain. The Frenchman's land is indeed his private domain and you enter upon it at your peril. The French will have the law on their side if they have to use force to evict you from their land, so be wary of pulling your caravan into what looks like an attractive field for the night without first asking permission.

Cinemas are to be found in most largish towns and they show a mixture of French and American/English films. The latter are usually dubbed into French so it can be amusing to watch the lips moving for the English dialogue while French words are coming out of the loudspeakers.

By the standards of the BBC, French television is second or third rate. It is broadcast on a different system so a UK set will not normally work unless it is dual PAL/SECAM. News and current affairs programmes are well informed and presented but there is no tradition of superb entertainment programmes, or of costume drama. There are both state and commercial channels with little to choose between them. Radio has proliferated in recent years and running your FM tuner across the dial will pick up a large range of broadcasts, mostly local.

It is possible to receive BBC TV transmissions using a special decoder for the satellite which can be obtained from a Swedish organization called TV Extra, Storgatan 9, 591 33 Sweden. There is an annual charge of about £70 plus a joining fee of £19 for your decoder card. If you are keen to be able to receive a particular satellite transmission in France, it is probably wisest to write to them to ask for advice on the size of antenna and frequencies and decode system necessary before spending on what may turn out to be an inappropriate set of equipment.

Sky TV can be picked up using the same equipment as used in Britain, but be warned: this is a breach of copyright.

PAL system VHS video recorders, as used in Britain, will not work in France unless they are connected to a PAL or PAL/SECAM television and are given PAL/VHS cassettes to play. If you wish to play British cassettes it is necessary to take out with you your entire apparatus of video player and television. The British PAL cassettes when played on a French SECAM system only play as black and white and all colour is lost. By the same token French cassettes, recorded on the SECAM system have to be played through a SECAM set-up. Some video recorders are dual standard PAL/SECAM and will work with PAL or SECAM tapes but they still need a television of the appropriate type or a dual system monitor. If in doubt, ask a knowledgeable dealer and, certainly, before spending any money on what you hope will be a workable combination.

Finally, but by no means of lesser importance, the BBC World Service can be picked up on the appropriate frequencies and, unless the campaign to save it has failed, Radio 4 can be picked up on the old long-wave frequency of 1500 metres, in all but the most southerly regions. World Service frequencies vary according to the time of day and the best, at any one time, will depend on climatic conditions. For a complete list of frequencies see the *Radio Times* or write to the BBC at Bush House, London WC2B 4PH.

Although fond of owning land, the French are not a nation of keen gardeners but, in contrast, many of their towns and villages are riots of colour with ornamental flower beds and tubs, hanging baskets and beautiful displays, maintained by both the authorities and private individuals. Nevertheless, garden centres are springing up in more and more locations and there are always the specialist growers of geraniums, which are by far the most popular window-box flower. The reason for this is simple as flies and mosquitoes are supposed to detest the smell of geranium leaves, so a window-box full of them is supposed to keep the house clear of these pests. As one would expect, the warmer and often drier climate favours many beautiful and attractive species of flower which find life difficult north of the English Channel, and likewise there are others which miss the damp and the cold and fail to thrive in the sun. Any good plantsman will be able to advise you, if it is important to know what to plant, but remember that, if watering is necessary, it can become something of a chore as well as expensive, depending on your source of supply. Remember Jean de Florette in the famous book of that name by Marcel Pagnol.

Newspapers follow a pattern similar to that in Britain, with a number of Paris-based papers which serve as national dailies and a proliferation of smaller local or regional papers. Among the former *Le Figaro* and *Le Monde* are reckoned, by some, to be among the best papers in the world. The largest circulation is achieved by the Rennes-based provincial daily *Ouest-France* which appears with numerous regional sub-editions.

For any aspiring French resident, the study of the newspapers, and particularly a well-written one such as *Le Figaro* or *Le Monde*, is a most useful exercise and one to be recommended. Try to set aside an hour per day to read a leading article in the paper, with a good dictionary such as the *Collins-Robert* by your side. Look up all the words you don't know, or are the least bit unsure of, and watch your command of the language improve within a few months. Read the rest of the paper and you will soon find yourself getting the gist of it. What you will find absent from the French press is the salacious reporting of personal and private lives and sex scandals which seem to have become so popular in the British tabloids of late. Investigative journalism is practised however, and frequently to good effect against politicians.

If your craving for an English paper is such that you must see one, they can often be found in the larger newsagents about a day old and at an inflated price. Supply seems to be erratic unless a regular order is placed. The price-hike is not usually a whim of the supplier but is the publisher's recommended overseas price which is printed on the front of the paper, so you can confirm that you aren't being taken for a ride by the newsagent by looking at the price panel.

Libraries are generally private and most sizeable towns have one. Obviously there won't be many books in English, if any at all. Similarly, you can't expect to find many English titles in the bookshops except specialist establishments in Paris. If you want a particular book in English, it is probably easiest to order it by post from the publisher, or get a friend to buy it and post it to you.

The predominant religion of France remains Roman Catholicism but, as in most European countries, religious observance is in decline, especially among the younger members of society, and few of the churches are well attended on a regular basis. Amalgamation of parishes and the establishment of team ministries are now commonplace and many churches are falling into a poor state of repair, due to a severe lack of funds. Anglican churches exist in a few places with attendant ministers but there are virtually no non-conformist churches at all. Many towns have on display, at the roadside on entry, a sign advertising the times of Mass in the parish church, and it is probably fair to say that the majority of babies are baptized into a faith which their parents are only lukewarm in following. Armistice Sunday is observed, almost universally, throughout the country with ceremonies at war memorials in villages and communes, and one notable feature of these is the active involvement of the children in the acts of remembrance for their forebears lost during the war. Ecumenism seems to be practised to the extent that an Anglican is welcome to enter a Roman church and join in worship, short of taking Communion if he or she wishes, with no questions asked or sideways looks given if an unfamiliarity with the liturgy is evident. The church has given the country some of its most spectacular buildings after the *châteaux* and it is sad to see so many of them falling into disrepair, but there seems to be no movement for their conversion into homes as is found in parts of Britain.

CHAPTER THIRTEEN

BON APPÉTIT

Virtually all dreams involving France include the pleasures of the table — after all it's what the French are most famous for and is probably one of the underlying reasons for going there. It is not my purpose to give you a guide to the guides, but there are almost as many guides to restaurants, each with its own grading system, as there are months in the year. They nearly all appear in English and can be bought in bookshops before you cross the Channel. You can get the juices flowing in advance, merely by studying the names of the establishments and their specialities. The word *auberge* will feature prominently because almost every other restaurant is the *auberge* of this or that.

The French are especially fond of eating out *en famille* for lunch on Sunday and it is always wise to make a reservation for this meal, and prudent to book for any meal at a popular restaurant.

The first thing to remember about eating in France is that it is intended to be enjoyable and is not something to be hurried. The French think nothing of spending three hours over lunch. If your idea of a meal out is to spend an hour or less shoving two or three courses down your throat as fast as you can and rushing off back to the car — or whatever else is next on your programme — then you are going to miss out on a great deal, as well as become very frustrated, as you champ at the bit waiting for the next course or the bill. Spend time really reading *la carte* and, for a start, look at both the fixed price offerings and the menu.

The *prix fixé* is exactly what its name implies — a fixed-price meal, often with considerable choice possible, for the same price and usually extremely good value. Most restaurants offer two or three different prices and a *menu de dégustation* which will be the most expensive and often beyond the capacity of all but the most dedicated trenchermen to enjoy to the full. What a lovely word *dégustation* is — it conjures up visions of sheer gluttony and over-indulgence.

The *à la carte* will be an extensive list of dishes, some of which will be marked *disponible* meaning that they may not necessarily be available if the ingredients are not in season or the *Chef de Cuisine* has not been able to get them at the right quality. This will often apply to seafood items in an inland restaurant.

While you are studying the menu it is common to be asked if you want an apéritif. A common choice is a *kir* which is white wine and cassis — blackcurrant concentrate — or, if preferred, with a peach juice — *un kir pêche*. The menu will usually be the same whether you are lunching or eating dinner. Regional specialities will usually figure in any restaurant and their sampling is part of the pleasure of eating out in France, but vegetables will not figure highly on any menu in a restaurant of any pretension — the French, while growing and eating the most delicious vegetables at home, do not expect to be offered what they consider to be the food of the poor when they dine out. It is a shame in my opinion but there it is. Most vegetables are included in the price of the main dish. If you come across dishes whose names you don't understand it is common for the owner to be able to translate, so don't be afraid to ask. After all you might miss out on an exceptional delicacy or delight for the lack of a simple question.

Another difference which can come as a surprise is the absence of silver service even in the high-class establishments. Nearly all meals are served already plated in the kitchen.

The wine list will have been offered to you with the menu. It will usually be self-explanatory and will often have maps to show the regions from which the wines on offer have come. In a high-class restaurant the wines will have been chosen from the *châteaux* by the *patron*, probably several years before, and can be expected to be of good quality. Lesser establishments will have bought from a merchant — *un négociant* — and, for a connoisseur, the quality may not be so good but it will usually be adequate. What will come as a surprise however is the price; wines in restaurants are expensive — frequently two or three times what you would expect to pay in the supermarket for virtually the same product. The mark-up on restaurant wines is frequently as much as 300% and tends to be higher on the cheaper wines so that they all end up expensive, with the superior wines being the better value. Unlike the UK, there is no tradition of customers taking along their own wine and paying corkage on it. You will just have to grin and bear it or go without, while taking consolation from the normally excellent value of the food.

When it comes to paying simply ask for *l'addition* or *la facture* and pay the bottom line amount. There is no need nowadays for tiresome calculations of 10% for service unless the words *Service non Compris* appear at the foot of the bill. VAT will have been included or will appear as a separate item within the total. The vast majority of restaurants accept credit cards.

You will probably be left to sit for as long as you like over your coffee or a *digestif* until you ask for the bill. Certainly don't expect to be booted out to make way for a second sitting of diners. Perhaps the nearest to an invitation to eat up and leave may be the appearance of the *patron* or the *Chef de Cuisine* in the body of the restaurant. If you have enjoyed your meal don't be shy of telling him, no matter how bad your French, he will understand and be flattered.

Most restaurants have no policy at all concerning smokers — there are too many addicts in France for them to risk alienating their patrons — so don't be surprised if someone lights up a Gauloise at the next table.

Above all, take your time and enter into the spirit of the event. Every meal out in France tends to be an event. Take to heart that lovely greeting, *bon appétit*.

Downstream of the restaurants as it were are the *crêperies* and *galetteries* selling mostly delicious *crêpes* and *galettes* in a profusion of flavours and fillings. These are much more than mere filled pancakes and can, quite easily, constitute a full meal for remarkably little money. They will be found in their mobile form at most street markets, as will stalls selling *saucissons* and pies. What you are less likely to find is the evil-smelling hot dog stall but they are beginning to make an appearance.

Markets are of course another of the particular delights of France. Virtually every town and village has a day of the week put aside for the regular street market where, depending on the size of the event, one may be able to buy almost anything. Vegetables will be in profusion, and all just as they came out of the ground and complete with earwigs in the cabbages, or ants among the beans. No cellophane or polyethylene wrapping here. Many of the vendors will be ordinary householders who have come to sell the odd few pounds of over-production from their garden or even the pickings from their nearest hedgerow at ridiculously low prices. Specialist garlic — *ail* — growers will be displaying their produce in all its wide variety of sizes and strengths in strings like onions.

The fresh fish stall is always worth a visit — its produce will be as fresh as is possible, having been caught the previous day and landed in the evening and the variety on offer is enormous. Shellfish will be in abundance too, lobsters, langoustines, mussels, crabs, cockles, all will be there.

There will be small producers of local cheese, often made from goat's milk (struggling to fight the tide of overwhelming bureaucracy emanating from Brussels which threatens to put them out of business) alongside large stalls selling a bewildering choice of commercially-made cheeses.

Animal rights activists are advised to keep their feelings in check as they enter the livestock area for here will be found chicks, ducklings, goslings, turkey chicks and the full grown versions of all these fowl in baskets, cardboard boxes and all manner of container. It is common to see the universal 2CV, conveying a pig in the front seat and a calf behind, as it bounces and bobs its way back to some smallholding out in the country.

For those still furnishing or doing-up their dream house, there will be beds and mattresses, kitchen implements, material for curtains, haberdashery, bed linen, bedside lamps, carpets and a wide choice of tools. In the larger markets there will also be a van where those who prefer to eschew the banking system can pay their phone bill, for among the smaller peasant farming community it is not so common to have a bank account.

Most markets are in full swing by about 9 a.m., are over and finished by noon, and by 2 p.m. the place will be spotlessly clean again with no sign of the frenetic activity of earlier hours.

Ordinary shops are little different to what one is used to in the UK but pharmacies are just that: don't expect to find pet food or photographic materials alongside the patent remedies. A pharmacy sells only pharmaceutical products and allied health requisites and there is usually only one in the smaller villages. Equally you can't buy medicines anywhere else except perhaps in a *droguerie*. Films are sold in tobacconists together with postage stamps, postcards, paperback books etc. The large supermarket chains (*Leclerc, Stoc, Super U, Shopi, Unico*, etc.) are all virtually carbon copies of Sainsbury's or Waitrose but sell a wider range of hardware lines and domestic equipment, including electrical goods and fittings, as well as clothes. Most shops shut for an hour or an hour-and-a-half for lunch, though some of the chains now stay open. Lunch is the main meal of the day for many French families and is taken all together at home.

The biggest difference between French and UK supermarkets is probably the range and price of wines on offer. In France it can be quite overwhelming. For the *cognoscenti* there are undoubted bargains to be found if they know their *appellations* and the years which are worth buying. If you see an undoubted bargain snap it up at once because the turn-over is very fast and it is unlikely that the stock will be there next day or even that afternoon. Chocolates, too, are an exceptional bargain; before Christmas the shelves will be laden with an enormous selection and all at what seem to be ridiculously low prices. Ground coffee is also cheap while paradoxically the instant variety is comparatively dear. It is definitely worth investing in a coffee-making machine of one sort or another — simple filter jugs are very cheap too. Another welcome feature is the ready availability of tinned vegetables in small sizes.

The supermarkets however have not yet supplanted the small specialist shops to the same extent as in the UK and neither have they killed off the village shop. *SPAR* and *Huit à Huit* support village enterprises throughout the country and most villages of any size have a butcher or even two, as well as the almost obligatory *boulanger* who may bake his bread twice a day so that it is always fresh. The *boulanger* will probably be a *pâtissier* as well, preparing and selling his own cakes and confections — sometimes to order. It is from him that you will buy your fresh *croissants* or *brioches* before strolling home through the wakening village to breakfast, having passed the time of day with the postman and other friends who were similarly up and about to get that lovely crusty bread which has no equal.

The butcher will deal with beef, mutton, lamb and their associated products while pork is the speciality of the *charcutier* and poultry is often sold in a specialist shop.

While the supermarkets carry a wide range of wines and it can be convenient to buy from them, to do so is to deny yourself one of the delights of France which is the seeking-out and buying of wines from the vineyard. Start by knowing the sort of wine you like and the area it comes from — things you will have found out over the years by examining the labels of bottles which you have particularly enjoyed. It can be worth keeping a small notebook in which to jot down the names of *châteaux* and *vignerons*. This will only be possible if you are drinking wine bottled by the producer — *mis en bouteilles à la propriété*. If it has been bottled by a merchant — *un négociant* — you will only get a clue to the area of the *appellation*. This is presupposing that you are drinking an *appellation controlée* wine rather than a blended product.

Having selected an area, the next thing to do is to go there and cruise around looking for signs offering tastings — *dégustations* — and of sales — *vente de vins*. There is no magic formula to apply in deciding which establishment to try. Personal recommendation is obviously a help, but otherwise it is a matter of luck.

The tasting is liable to be in a room specially set aside for the purpose where you will be surrounded by the owner's pension fund in the shape of a collection of dusty bottles containing old and rare vintages, but equally it may be in the cellar, where the wines are actually produced, and you will be surrounded by the enormous vats and barrels of the business. In either surroundings, the event can be as much fun and as pleasurable as you wish. You will be offered a choice of the wines produced by the vineyard and samples of any you choose to try. The *vigneron* will usually tell you something about the history of the vineyard, the *appellation*, the qualities of the various vintages and he will try to help you make your choice. He will also advise whether a wine is one to lay down for the future or one that cannot be expected to improve with age. If he is good at his job, he will not necessarily press you to buy the most expensive of his wines, but will normally expect you to buy enough bottles to make his effort in entertaining you worthwhile. Half a dozen bottles will do, but if you buy in bulk — say two dozen or more — you can hope for a discount. The cheapest way to buy is in bulk — *en vrac*. Bulk containers called *cubiténaires* of 25 or 50 litres can be bought for home-bottling, and often the *vigneron* will sell you the bottles and certainly the labels to put on them after you have filled and corked them. For the *cognoscenti*, this is undoubtedly the way to get superb wines at bargain prices; and there is a rare satisfaction in producing the bottles from your own cellar and telling the story of how you found the vineyard, chose the wine, brought it home and bottled it.

At the tasting, while it is undoubtedly possible, it is not necessary to get drunk because there will always be a spitoon and there is no disgrace in using it. The French are sympathetic to the fact that you are driving and will respect your desire to stay sober. At a good establishment you will be offered something to cleanse the palate between tastings, but beware of anything salty as this can hide the bitterness or sharpness of a wine which might be better sold as paint stripper.

Once you have discovered a *vigneron* whose wines you like, it can be nice to develop a loyalty and to return and buy from him again. He will remember you and a friendship may develop. Equally, if you like his wine, recommend him to friends. Personal knowledge is valuable as many smaller producers rely on their sales direct from the chateau because they can't always produce enough of any particular vintage to make it worthwhile for a supermarket to buy from them.

Small can most definitely be beautiful in the wine business and the only regrets you may have will come as you drink the last bottle of a favourite and now unobtainable vintage. Savour it and *bon appétit*.

CHAPTER FOURTEEN

HEALTHY, WEALTHY AND WISE

In the first flush of enthusiasm, for France and all things French, it is easy to overlook the fact that as your age increases, the problems of health and health care will loom ever more important in your life. We in Britain are used to a cradle-to-grave, free and all-embracing health service which — complain about it though we will — is still the envy of most of continental Europe.

If you are non-resident in France you can transport most of the benefits of the British system with you as you can receive free treatment, or the reimbursement of any expenses you have incurred abroad, by taking with you a form E111 obtainable from any post office. It is also advisable to take leaflet T4 entitled *Health Advice for Travellers*, with you as it contains detailed relevant advice. This is a Department of Health publication and can be obtained by ringing 0800 555 777 free at any time.

It is, nevertheless, necessary to understand a little of the French system in order to avoid booking in to a private sector hospital when the E111 only covers treatment in a public sector establishment.

French citizens pay into a scheme called *Sécurité Sociale* which roughly equates to our National Insurance. Subscriptions are made by employers and employees and are deducted at source from wages or salaries. The self-employed pay pro-rata to their income tax. These payments entitle the citizen to free treatment at any hospital, or by any doctor or dentist, within the system — *conventionné* — and there will be such a hospital and doctors in every major centre. The treatment will be adequate but the surroundings may not be so smart. For this reason, there exists a second tier of hospitals and practitioners whose fees will only partly be met by *Sécurité*

Sociale or maybe not at all. The rest is up to the patient. The degree by which they exceed *Sécurité Sociale* rates will vary and are always advertised — some will cost a lot more, others less so. The topping-up is usually done by membership of a scheme similar to BUPA or PPP called a *mutuelle*. *Mutuelles* are organized and run by most trade and professional organizations, for those plying the trade, and they take a subscription from their members. Unless you are a member of a comparable insurance scheme which covers you abroad, it is important to make sure that you only seek treatment from the *conventionné* sector, or there may be an unwelcome bill to pay at the end which the E111 will not cover. Such insurance will also commonly pay for repatriation if necessary and this could be very expensive if it involves air travel. Costs of repatriation are virtually never borne by the E111. Centurion Assistance operated by American Express is just one such scheme and there are many more. The motoring organizations will offer you health cover if you are effecting one of their overseas motoring insurances to cover you against breakdown on the road. An especially good service is provided by SOS and details can be obtained from Private Patients Plan on 0800 335555. Whatever scheme you choose, remember that reimbursement of charges is retrospective, so you will need to be able to pay them out of your own resources at the time the bills are presented.

If you have become resident in France and are of retirement age, then you are automatically covered by *Sécurité Sociale* for their basic level, so it could be worth taking out a top-up insurance policy to deal with any extras. A form E121 will be necessary when you register with *Sécurité Sociale* as proof of your status and eligibility as a pensioner in Britain.

The payments from *Sécurité Sociale* are graded according to the severity of the ailment being treated, so that full costs of treatment are reimbursed in the case of some diseases and illnesses, while others attract only partial cover. Not all the French fully understand their own system so it is small wonder that a foreigner will experience a similar problem.

If you are working, then it is imperative that you join *Sécurité Sociale* and pay your dues. A responsible employer will keep you on the straight and narrow but the temptation, if self-employed, to save the subscriptions which are based on your taxable income must be resisted. Don't try to use an E111 to obtain treatment for a broken arm sustained when falling from scaffolding around a house you are doing up for a friend. It only covers travellers in the country for less than six months and the authorities will soon smell a rat and come down on you. If eligible to join a *mutuelle*, it is common sense to do so and gain the extra peace of mind that it will bring. The *Chambre des Métiers* or the Chamber of Commerce — *Syndicat d'Initiative* — will be able to direct you to an appropriate *mutuelle* for your trade.

Ambulances in France are generally private and operated by the taxi firms. They are usually far less sophisticated than those which we are used to and certainly don't come near to 'casualty' standard, being mere conveyances for the sick and, as such, are frequently based on estate car bodies. Genuine emergency ambulances are summoned via the police by ringing 17 or 18, whereas the rest are arranged with the firm operating them.

Few French doctors will speak English well enough to understand your description of obstruse symptoms. Few of us will be able to translate the nuances of our ache or pain or malaise into understandable French, so any visit to the doctor is going to be difficult. The more popular resorts on the Côte d'Azur will have a handful of English-speaking doctors but they are likely to be outside the *Sécurité Sociale* system and a visit will need to be prearranged with an appropriate IMF loan. There is an American-based organization called IAMAT which aims to provide English-speaking medical assistance to travellers and which has about 30 doctors registered in France. They can be contacted on 93 88 42 14, but remember that they are definitely not *conventionné*.

Perhaps the best advice one can give is to stay healthy. The climate and the good food will help but when they fail and you fall ill, perhaps the best place to be is back home in Britain in the arms of the NHS.

CHAPTER FIFTEEN

SIGNING ON THE DOTTED LINE

Earlier chapters have covered the importance of the decision whether or not to become a full-time resident in France, and some of the implications of doing so. This chapter sets out some of the steps along the road for those who decide to take the plunge, and some of the procedures which it will be necessary for them to follow as their life in France continues, perhaps to its end.

Taking up residence is a big step and not to be undertaken lightly because of the implications for your tax status, your health care, your motoring costs and the general commitment which it entails.

The routine to be followed differs slightly, depending on whether or not you are of retirement age and, if below it, on whether or not you intend to work in France.

Persons of independent means who are British citizens and who do not intend to work in France must apply for a permanent residence visa — *la visa d'établissement* — from the French consulate. This category includes the retired as well as those who have enough wealth that they do not need to work. Proof of your adequacy of means will be needed. The visa should be obtained before final departure for your new home and can take several months to be processed, so apply in good time. Your British passport, which must confirm your British citizenship, must be a full one and not a temporary or visitor's passport. Those who intend to work do not need to obtain this visa.

Once installed in France and living in your own or a rented home, regardless of whether or not you are working, you must apply for a residence permit — *une carte de séjour*. This is applied for initially at the local *mairie* or *préfecture*. The officials may not use a standard procedure throughout the country but you will certainly need to produce your passport, three passport size photographs, birth and marriage certificates as appropriate. Where necessary, these should be translated into French by an authorized translator. (The consulate will give you a list of authorized translators and it is wise to get the translation done before departure from Britain.) Finally you must be able to show that you have a roof to live under, in the shape of a rent receipt or, if you have purchased, a certificate from the notary to the effect that you own a house. Additionally, if working, you must be able to prove the fact by means of a pay slip or other document. If not working, you must be able to show evidence of your means and ability to support yourself. It is also worth being able to tell anyone who asks, the names and places of birth and birthdays of parents and grandparents. It may even be necessary to be able to give evidence that you don't have a criminal record, and to show that you are in good health. It can all depend on the whim of the official dealing with an application, and on the local attitude to incomers. Expect more hassle if you represent a potential threat to the local unemployed by seeking the same work as them. The EEC pundits may have declared the labour market to be free but the French in some areas have different ideas and will seek to protect their interests.

Having got your precious residence permit, carry it with you at all times; it is your identity card as far as the French are concerned. Until you get it, carry your passport.

The residence permit must be obtained within one year of arrival and will probably need to be renewed after 12 months, when you can hope to be given one that will last for five years.

Don't mistake residence for citizenship. Unless you take the very positive step of acquiring French nationality you will remain a British citizen for life, albeit living as a resident in a foreign country. For this reason it is strongly recommended that you take the trouble to register your presence with the nearest British consulate. The chances of needing their active intervention are remote in the extreme but they will always be able to locate you in an emergency if the folks back home have lost touch. Imagine losing an inheritance because you were so well tucked away in deepest rural France that no-one could find you!

Having become established let us suppose that you have fallen for one of the locals in a big way and wish to get married. The formalities of marriage are similar to those in Britain except that it is only the civil ceremony which has any legal significance. Even if married in church it is necessary to go through the civil proceedings beforehand. As with so much else, the first port of call is the *mairie* of the district where one of you lives, or has lived for at least a month. Once again your residence permit will be needed and this time they are going to want to see your birth certificate which must bear the stamp of the nearest British consulate and also a medical certificate obtained in France within the previous two months. If you have been married before it will be necessary to show either your divorce certificate or the death certificate of your former spouse (again translated into French by an approved translator and stamped by the consulate). If marrying a widow be warned that French law prohibits her remarriage within 300 days of the death of the former spouse, and that a similar prohibition applies to a divorcee. Either ban can be got around by obtaining a certificate from a doctor to the effect that the lady is not pregnant. If she gives birth during the 300 days her child is deemed to have been fathered by her deceased or former husband so shotgun weddings can misfire. The town hall will publish your banns of marriage for ten days, both at the town hall where you are to be married and also where you are each residing, if different. At the ceremony each of you must bring at least one and not more than two witnesses, whose names will have been declared to the town hall when making your first application. Your marriage will be recognized virtually anywhere in the world.

When they marry, French women do not necessarily assume the surname of their husband and continue to use their maiden name in official documents where a lady will be described as Madame (maiden name), wife of M. (husband's name). Whether a woman uses her married or maiden name is entirely up to her.

When you marry you will be given a kind of family logbook

called *un livret de famille* in which you are legally obliged to record all births, deaths and other events taking place within your family, including divorce. Unless you and your spouse have drawn up a special contract specifying otherwise, your assets in France or elsewhere, owned prior to your marriage, remain your individual property, as do any which you inherit after it. Belongings acquired by you and/or your spouse after your marriage belong to you both jointly and will have to be divided between you if you divorce or separate.

The French also recognize cohabitation by issuing certificates of *concubinage*. Despite its romantic sound with echoes of the *Arabian Nights* this does little more than acknowledge that Mr A and Mlle B have decided to live together. It doesn't confer on either party the rights enjoyed by a legally married spouse and a concubine is assessed at 60% for inheritance tax. The certificate is issued by the town hall and almost its only benefit is that it does entitle its holders to family railcards on *SNCF*.

If the marriage, or any other which was in being when you moved to France, doesn't work out then you may contemplate divorce. To obtain a divorce in France, it is necessary to be married to a French national or for both parties to be resident in France. It is also necessary to use the services of a lawyer. A quick divorce can be obtained after not less than six months of marriage if both partners are in agreement over details for the division of assets, arrangements for children, finance, etc. Provided both parties still agree, the divorce is granted three months after the application has been made and is heard by a judge.

If the parties are not in agreement then the case will be heard by a court. Six years' separation or mental illness are usually taken as grounds for divorce but it may be refused if the court considers that it will have an adverse effect on the ill party or on children of the marriage, having regard to their age and circumstances. Maintenance, etc., is determined, as in Britain, but the French have set a lead which we in Britain are only just following with the Child Support Agency, in being strict in enforcing the payment of maintenance and keeping partners informed of each other's whereabouts.

If, on the other hand, as one would hope, your marriage is

a success and the sunshine and French ambience work their magic, then maybe you will have a child born in France. Births must be registered at the town hall of the district in which they occur and within three working days of the event. A birth certificate will have been issued by the doctor or midwife attending the mother and this must be produced when the birth is registered. If you wish your child to be eligible for a British passport, it is also essential that the birth be registered with the nearest British Consulate. Your child will automatically qualify for British citizenship if both parents are British; it only becomes a French national if at least one parent is French by birth.

If the grim reaper comes to call and a death takes place, once again there are formalities to be followed. Deaths must be registered at the town hall within 24 hours. A death certificate will have been issued by the doctor attending the patient or, if death was sudden and unexpected, by the practitioner who attended him or her. Death certificates do not state the cause of death. Arrangements for funerals are, strange as it may seem to the British, a responsibility of the local authority who will instruct a local undertaker or give you permission to do so. The coffin may not be closed for at least 24 hours and neither may it remain open for more than six days after the death. If you wish it to be closed earlier than just before the funeral it may be necessary to give the undertaker specific instructions on this point as it is customary for the closing to be left as late as reasonably practicable so that relatives and friends can pay their last respects.

Cemeteries are non-denominational and so a Protestant can be buried in one just as readily as a Roman Catholic. Cremation is growing in acceptance but it is necessary for the deceased to have left a letter stating the desire to be cremated. Crematoria are not very thick on the ground but more are being built as the practice gains in popularity. For the religious side of the funeral it will be necessary to contact the appropriate minister of the faith concerned. There are Anglican ministers and churches in several parts of France and, if this is of importance to you, it will be as well to have made contact with him before you need his services in a hurry as it were.

If you wish to repatriate the deceased's remains for burial

in Britain, remember that it will be expensive and something of a bureaucratic obstacle course. Your first port of call, if you wish to do it, will be the nearest consulate who will advise you on the formalities required. It might be simpler, if within the spirit of the deceased's wishes, to have a cremation in France and then to bring the ashes home for interment or scattering — or whatever is wished.

If you have children, or you are taking children of school age to France with you whom you wish to educate there, it is as well to know a little about the French education system. The French count school years backwards from the final year at the end of what we would regard as secondary education, at the age of 18. Thus the first year's schooling is in the twelfth grade — *douzième* — and starts at the age of about five in a kindergarten — *école maternelle*. Next, covering from the tenth to around the fifth is the primary school — *école primaire* — which is followed by the secondary school — *collège d'enseignement secondaire* or *CES. CES* is comprehensive in character but streamed and lasts up to the third grade when pupils destined for university go on to the *lycée* and the less academically gifted go to technical college — *lycée profesionnel* — or are indentured to a trade. As stated earlier, the French maintain a tradition of respect for artisan skills and virtually all trades have a training and qualification scheme similar to our now largely discontinued apprenticeship.

In the *lycée* the pupils study for the *baccalauréat* which is a course and examination regime in two parts. The first year is common to all and deals with French language and literature. The second year offers a choice and is a course which is specialized in content and which will normally lead to university entrance or to one of the professions, according to which of the options is taken.

All tuition is free, but books and stationery have to be bought, second-hand if needs be. Most French schools treat their pupils in a more adult manner than we are accustomed to, and expect the pupils to respond in like manner by behaving responsibly. There is no mollycoddling of the lazy or giving of second chances to failures. Academic competition is encouraged at every turn. Any English-speaking child of more than about seven or eight, entering the system, would find it very hard to flourish unless particularly gifted and fluent in French. Conversely it is probable that a child joining the system for, say, a year of secondary education would gain immense benefit from the experience and would become truly bi-lingual.

There are a very few English-speaking schools but the most notable is the English School in Paris.

Private (fee-paying) schools exist and are considered to give an education inferior to that of the state schools. They are mostly linked to religious foundations and many offer boarding, which is uncommon in France.

The school year is somewhat different to ours in that the Christmas and Easter holidays are shorter but the summer break can last for as long as three months. Saturday school is the norm at present.

University is followed by post-graduate studies at a *grande école* and a degree is a necessary prerequisite for the majority of professions and for the civil service. All men must do a spell of National Service between *lycée* and university or after their technical school.

As with our own educational system, the scene in France is ever-changing in response to changes in society. There is a greater emphasis and encouragement on engineering and technical skills in the schools which is mirrored by the greater status accorded to the engineer in French society; even the artisan tradesman is respected more than seems to be the case in Britain, but the prospects for many school leavers at the moment are no more encouraging than here.

TOUT COMPLET

The sun has dipped behind the distant hills leaving only the warmth radiating from the stone walls as a reminder of the heat of the day. Under a clear sky, the air temperature falls and dew forms on the grass. A light mist rises into a veil over the river almost hiding a family of ducks paddling quietly over from their daytime dabbling spot to snap up the leftover bits of *baguette* from our lunch.

In the distance a church bell rings the hour for the second time at five past, lest it was missed on the hour. A flock of pigeons flap past looking for their evening roost and from the kitchen comes an unforgettable aroma of herbs, garlic, butter and all things tasty, as supper is bubbling gently in the slow cooker.

Tomorrow will probably be another lovely sunny day — perhaps we'll go over to Sainte Suzanne to the brocante fair and lunch in that little restaurant by the church. It's the annual fair in the village downriver and in the evening there will be the funfair and the fireworks to watch from the riverbank while enjoying a picnic under the poplars on the edge of the water.

For now I am happy to enjoy a *kir pêche* and to revel in the peace, which is hardly disturbed by the passing of some villagers on their evening stroll with their dog. *'Bonsoir Messieurs Dame — qu'il a fait beau aujourd'hui.'* A few words of social chat and they continue their walk. This was the dream and it came true and has endured. I wouldn't change it for worlds. May your dream come equally true.

USEFUL INFORMATION

Estate Agents Operating Across the Channel:

Properties in France, 34 Imperial Terrace, Cheltenham, Glos., GL50 1QZ. Tel. 01242 253848

Homes in Real France, 3 Delgany Villas, Plymouth, PL6 8AG. Tel. 01752 771777 (Tel. or Fax)

The French Retreat, 82–84 Vauxhall Street, Barbican, Plymouth, PL4 0EX. Tel. 01752 266220 (Proprietor, Tony Cremer-Price. Properties in Brittany — full service).

John and Ruth Reid (Poitou Charente region) Tel. (France) 49 87 39 85. Fax 49 87 92 46.

French Discoveries, Tregonhay, St Dominick, Saltash, Cornwall, PL12 6TE. Tel. 01579 50162. Fax 01579 50262.

Maison Secondaire, 96 Westernlea, Crediton, Devon, EX17 3JE. Tel. 01363 774825 (Fax also).

Sinclair Overseas Property Network, P.O. Box 429, Leighton Buzzard, Beds, LU7 7WG. Tel. 01525 375319. Fax 01525 375319.

Rutherfords, 25 Vanstone Place, London, SW6 1AZ. Tel. 0171 386 9826. Fax 0171 386 5122.

Alliance, 1 Hawthorn Road, Wallington, Surrey, SM6 0SX. Tel. 0181 669 6576. Fax 0181 669 5980.

Vivre en France, 47 Bulwer Road, Leytonstone, London, E11 1DE. Tel. 0181 558 3016. Fax 0181 669 5980.

Listings of French Properties for Sale:

Living France, 9 High Street South, Olney, Bucks, MK46 4AA. Tel. 01234 240954.

French Property News, 2a Lambton Road, Raynes Park, London SW20 0LR. Tel. 0181 944 5500. Fax 0181 944 5293.

Notaires' Scale Fees:

Cost of property	Fee percentage
0 to 20,000 francs	5
20,000 to 40,000 francs	3.3
40,000 to 110,000 francs	1.65
Above 110,000 francs	0.825

Stamp Duty:

On a property bought as a private residence and certified as such in the *Acte de Vente* — between 5 and 6% variable according to region.

Land Registry Fees:

Approximately 8%.

Agent's Fees:

Cost of property	Fee percentage
0 to 50,000 francs	8
50,000 to 100,000 francs	7
100,000 to 150,000 francs	6
150,000 to 350,000 francs	5
350,000 to 700,000 francs	4
Above 700,000 francs	By negotiation

If the Notaire Acted as Agent:

On the first 175,000 francs — 5%. On the excess over 175,000 francs — 2.5%.

Consulates:

The British Embassy, Consular Section, 9 Avenue Hoche, 75008 Paris. Tel. (Paris) 42 66 38 10.

There are consulates in the following towns and cities:

Cedex		Telephone
33001	Bordeaux	56 52 28 35
62201	Boulogne	21 30 25 15
62100	Calais	21 34 45 48
59377	Dunkirk	28 66 11 98
51200	Epernay	26 51 31 02
76600	Le Havre	35 42 27 47
59800	Lille	20 52 87 90
69288	Lyon	78 37 59 67
13006	Marseille	91 53 43 32
44009	Nantes	40 48 57 47
06000	Nice	93 82 32 04
66000	Perpignan	68 34 56 99

French Authorities in Britain:

French Embassy, 58 Knightsbridge, London, SW1. Tel. 0171 235 8080.

French Consular Section and Cultural Department, 21–23 Cromwell Road, London, SW7. Tel. 0171 838 2000.

French Visa Applications, 6a Cromwell Place, P.O. Box 57, London, SW7 2EW.

French Government Tourist Office, 178 Piccadilly, London, W1V 0AL. Tel. 0171 629 1272.

The French Industrial Development Board, DATAR, 21–24 Grosvenor Place, London, SW1X 7HU. Tel. 0171 823 1895.

Useful British Organizations:

BBC World Service, P.O. Box 76, Bush House, Strand, London, WC2B 4PH. Tel. 0171 240 3456.

DSS Overseas Section, Venton Park, Newcastle-upon-Tyne, NE98 1YX. Tel. 0191 213 5000.

Inland Revenue Information Office, Citygate House, 39–45 Finsbury Park, London, EC2A 1HH. Tel. 0171 588 4226.

AA St John Alert, Fanum House, Basingstoke, Hants., RG21 2BR. Tel. 01256 24872.

Private Patients Plan, PPP House, Upperton Road, Eastbourne, East Sussex, BN21 1LH. Tel. 0800 335555.

Tax and Financial Planning and Advice

Blackstone Franks, Barbican House, 26–34 Old Street, London, EC1V 9HL. Tel. 0171 250 3300. Fax 0171 250 1402.

Other Useful Sources of Information and Help:

France Magazine Ltd, France House, Stow on the Wold, Glos., GL54 1BN. Tel. 01451 870871. *France Magazine* (published quarterly, by subscription). Interesting articles on France and French life, plus many adverts for services such as house-sitting, transport, etc., and properties for sale and to rent for holidays.

France House, Digbeth Road, Stow on the Wold, Glos., GL54 1BN. Tel. 01451 870871. Fax 01451 830869. All sorts of publications on France, including IGN maps, guides, posters, language cassettes, etc., can be purchased from France House.

Thrings and Long, Solicitors, Midland Bridge, Bath, Avon, BA1 2HQ. Tel. 01225 448494. Fax 01225 319735.

Weekend Courses for First Time Buyers in France, provided by A. and L. Webb, Cowleaze Paddock, Hartham, Corsham, Wilts., SN13 0PZ. Tel. 01249 713179.

Consultancy in France, Wickham Farm, Marston Magna, Yeovil, Somerset, BA22 8DT. Tel. 01935 850274. Fax 01935 851166.

Ferry Companies:

Brittany Ferries, Millbay Docks, Plymouth. Tel. 01752 269926 for timetable. Tel. 01705 827701 for reservations. Brittany Ferries offer reductions to owners of French property who join their club.

P&O European Ferries. Tel. 01304 203388.

Stena-Sealink. Tel. 01233 647047.

Hoverspeed. Tel. 01304 240241.

The Shuttle. Tel. 0990 353535.

GLOSSARY

A discuter: For negotiation or discussion
A louer: For hire or to rent
A péage: To be paid for; toll payable
A restaurer: For restoration
Agent: Policeman
Assainissement: Main drains

Boules: The game of pétanque
Bricolage: Building/repair/DIY

Certificat d'Urbanisme: Town planning charter
Chai: Wine cellar (for production)
Chambre d'Hôte: Bed and breakfast
Chauffe-eau: Water heater
Compromis de Vente: Contract of sale
Constat à l'amiable: Accident statement
Conventionée (hôpital):   In the state system
Courtier: Broker
Crépi: Decorative plaster finish

Devis: Estimate
Disjoncteur: Earth leakage/overload trip
Donation entre époux: Gift between spouses

Eaux usées: Drain water
Entretien: Maintenance
Etang: Lake or pond

Fermette: Smallholding
Flics: Policemen (slang)
Fosse septique: Septic tank
Frais: Fees

Gendarme: Member of National Guard
Geomètre: Surveyor
Gîte: Self-catering accommodation
Grenier: Attic or loft

Heures creuses: Off-peak electricity
Heures pleines: Full rate electricity

Hôtel de Ville: Town hall
Huissier: Loss or claims adjuster

Immobilier: Estate agent

Livraison: Delivery

Maire: Mayor
Mairie: Administrative office of the Mayor
Mas: House in the Provençal style

Notaire: Notary

Patrimoine: Cultural heritage
Permis de construire: Planning permission
Poubelle(s):   Dustbin/rubbish collection
Puissance: Power rating

Randonnées: Walks or excursions (foot or cycle)

Sécurité sociale: Social security
Servitudes: Building regulations
SNCF: French state railways

Taxe d'habitation: Rates
Tax Foncière: Council tax/community charge
Trésor public: Public treasury/treasurer's department
TGV: High-speed train

Usufruit: Legal term relating to inheritance

Vignette: Car tax disc/certificate
Vignette d'assurance: Car insurance certificate

POSTSCRIPT

In January 1995 it rained incessantly for several weeks in western France and most of the larger rivers burst their banks and flooded much of the countryside.

It was Wednesday morning when our telephone rang at our home in England and Archie, one of our neighbours in France, told me that the river outside our house was about to enter the building. He and Rosemary had lifted up the carpet in the living room and the fire brigade had been along with concrete blocks onto which they had lifted the fridge and the cooker and the dehumidifier. All we could do was to sit back and pray that the river would stop rising.

The river continued to rise for the next three days and reached the height of our kitchen worktops, covering their tiles. There it remained for a couple of days before dropping and returning to floor level. Rosemary and Archie were evacuated by punt, together with Monsieur Messier, their neighbour, and friendly French families took them in.

The authorities were swift to act and, before the water had subsided, our village had been declared a natural disaster area and ourselves as *Sinistres*. This meant that public funds would be available for relief and repair, even if those making a claim were not covered by insurance or if, as in our case, the insurance cover specifically excluded flood damage. There was an explanatory leaflet in the post and this was soon followed by a form to be completed and returned to the *Mairie* as soon as possible. This had to describe the damage to house and contents, supported by estimates of the cost of repair or replacement together with estimates where appropriate.

I went out to France exactly a week after the inundation, arriving late in the morning on a fine sunny day. On arrival, after the usual pleasantries of meeting (four pecks for

Rosemary and Maryse because they are very special), I surveyed the damage. The fire brigade had been in again and had hosed out the mud from the main rooms downstairs, leaving only the loo untouched so that I could see the extent of the damage.

I set to cleaning up the kitchen units and their drawers which, being made of melamine-faced chipboard, would suffer from swelling the longer they were left. Amazingly they had survived remarkably well; a tribute to Texas from whom they were bought. The floors, being tiled as is normal in France, had not suffered at all and wiped clean, though water continued to ooze from the joints for a few days. Whether from design or by chance I know not, but our electrical installation was such that all the sockets and wiring except the convector heaters were above the high water mark, so I was able to put power on immediately, a circuit at a time, and the fuses held in until I got to the cooker. A fan heater was rigged up and directed at its switches for a couple of hours, and then at the convector heaters.

The fridge had floated around, but halfway through the afternoon the fire brigade returned and hosed out both the loo and the fridge which was found to be working. At the end of the day I set the dehumidifier to work, together with a second one I had taken out with me. They extracted at their maximum rate, assisted by a little heat, and the only other work to be done in the house was to demount the panelling of the kitchen and living room so that the wood of which it was made could dry out.

I tell this story mainly to point out the benefits of solid tiled floors, of having good neighbours and of a sensible electrical installation above flood level. I must also pay tribute to the unbelievable kindness and friendliness of all the rest of the villagers. I was beset with offers of help to clean up which came from people I hardly knew. The fire brigade were magnificent, both before and afterwards. It turned out that one of the firemen thought he recognized me and, after a lot of head scratching, we realized that his normal job was that of lock-keeper. The flood had overwhelmed his lock and so he had teamed up with the emergency services. He remembered me from when my boat passed through his lock in the summer.

Above all, I was impressed by the speed and sympathy of the official response which showed the truly local nature of French local government. The village *mairie* had power to act and did so immediately it was give the 'Go ahead' by Ministerial pronouncement and delegation from the *prefecture.*

As it turned out, the damage to our house was so trivial that it wasn't worth claiming the relief funds. Others had far greater need of the money than us because many businesses and shops were flooded in the nearby town.

The last time the river had reached such a height was back in the 1930s or earlier and, in retrospect, my greatest regret is that I waited until the flood had gone down before I went out, and so didn't actually see it.

Far from making us want to sell up and move, the experience has merely strengthened our love of the village and I am now slowly rebuilding the kitchen using marine ply instead of chipboard.

It has been suggested to me that as our floors are solid and we have only one door, it might be feasible to prevent water ingress merely by sealing up the front door and turning the whole house into a sort of cofferdam.

The secret of drying out is ventilation or use of a dehumidifier. If using a dehumidifier it will work better if you can also heat up the air a bit but care is needed if this is not to cause trouble elsewhere in the house, particularly upstairs, through condensation. The warm humid air from lower floors is liable to rise and condense on any cool surface.

The river has now resumed its normal innocent appearance and the weir is roaring again as the water cascades down the slope. The silence when it was drowned was quite uncanny and I hope never to meet it again.